ROBERTA M. STARRY has explored, painted, photographed, and written about the California, Arizona, and Nevada back-country for the past twenty-five years. She also gives talks to students, youth groups, and museum members on the history, geology, and flora of the eastern Kern County.

Rand area correspondent for *The Bakersfield Californian,* Roberta Starry's articles and photos have appeared in many publications, including *The Christian Science Monitor, Desert Magazine, The West,* and *National Parks Magazine.* She has won numerous desert painting awards, photo awards, and most recently, First Place for historic articles in the California Press Women's Contest in 1972.

THE WARD RITCHIE PRESS

# EXPLORING THE GHOST TOWN DESERT

BY ROBERTA MARTIN STARRY

*Dedicated to my brother Edwin,*
*the desert explorer par excellence.*

*The material in this book is reviewed and updated*
*at each printing.*

TITLE PAGE: *Old Sunshine Mine at Randsburg.*

# CONTENTS

*Randsburg has changed little since this photo was taken 40 years ago. The effect of the cut back in mining was already shrinking the mining community.*

# INTRODUCTION

U.S. Highway 395 bisects the fabulous Rand Mining area approximately one hundred and fifty miles north of Los Angeles and serves as the main street of the diminutive communities of Atolia, Red Mountain and Johannesburg. Randsburg, where the big mining boom originated, is but a short distance off the highway seen clinging to the mountain side below the one time great gold producing Yellow Aster Mine.

Rand area in the Mojave Desert has an exciting yet well balanced mixture of sand, rock, rugged mountain ranges and colorful canyons interlaced with old trails, abandoned prospects and crumbling buildings. Through each mile runs an invisible thread that ties the present to a romantic past of freighters, prospectors, investors, gamblers and pretty dance hall girls.

The flavor of those old days is still around, in a lesser degree as the years pass, but for those who pause to look, listen and feel, there is an illusive something from back in time. Adventure waits just around the curve of a dusty trail and challenging mountains hold wealth yet to be discovered.

A hundred years ago prospectors hiked and rock sampled their way along the foothills and canyons of the mineralized El Paso Mountains. Their search did not always produce gold but it did compensate with ability to survive in an arid land, outwit the lawless and add to the understanding of geology. It was a lonely life measured against today's standards.

The first exciting gold discovery to draw public attention to this area was made in a gulch opening into Fremont Valley, on the eastern side of the El Paso Range. Forty-four years earlier, an emigrant named Goler had seen nuggets somewhere in this locality while making his way from Death Valley to the Los Angeles area. Starved, weak, and frightened of Indians, Goler hurried south, with plans of someday returning to claim the gold. Investors believed the story and financed several searches, none with any degree of success.

The narrow canyon of the 1893 strike became known as Goler. There were those that believed it was the lost gold site; others passed the idea off as miner's talk and went on searching for a bigger strike. Whether Goler saw this place or not was of little concern as excitement over the find mounted. Glamour of the Mother Lode in northern California was about gone and prospectors were frantically searching for a rich new field.

Word of the strike spread fast, men arrived in droves and grabbed any claim they could get. Considering the slow transportation of that time, plus the total lack of phones or other means of communication, the speed with which news of gold traveled is still one of the unexplained wonders of the desert. Miners of the early Rand years credit the sage brush telegraph and jack rabbit gossip for the fast news coverage.

Restlessness, a characteristic of prospectors, was probably the greatest factor in new discoveries. Summit Diggings a few miles to the east of Goler was producing well but prospectors moved back and forth between the two camps always searching for that big bonanza.

In 1895 three men who had periodically moved between the Goler and Summit operations decided to make one last search for gold before quitting their profitless mining venture. They left the Summit Diggings after telling friends that they were going to make one more try on their Goler claims but actually turned west toward a mountain that had been bypassed by prospectors as showing no sign of mineralization.

For F. M. Mooers, John Singleton and Charles Burcham, their

last prospecting effort was their best. The colorless, uninteresting mountain made them millionaires.

At the first sign of gold the three prospectors had frantically set about staking as many claims as possible before anyone learned of the discovery. Like Goler it was only a matter of a few hours before men began arriving, marking off claims and setting up their camps.

Rand Camp started as one tent, but quickly progressed to a tent, wagon-box and board city that burned to the ground twice within a few weeks. Undaunted by lack of water, primitive living conditions and baffling desert weather, men poured in and a boom was on. High pitched laughter and piano music echoed in the saloon-lined streets, competing with lodge meetings and opera-house entertainment.

Down in Fremont Valley a small settlement known as Cow Wells had been little more than a cow watering place and a way station for freighters on the long haul to and from the Panamint mines west of Death Valley. Goler and Rand Camp's Yellow Aster gold, hauled to Eugene Garlock's mill at Cow Wells, boomed the settlement in the valley, changed its name to Garlock and made it a favored rest stop for miner, business man, greenhorn, gambler or family enroute to the gold fields. Hotels offered good beds, home cooked food, and the latest gold news. Saloons washed away the dust of stage coach miles, a rough freight wagon trip or a long hike in from the mountains with a poke of gold. Corrals and stables housed weary teams while drivers relaxed, a one man laundry kept the miners clean and slaughter house provided the whole area with fresh meat—as fresh as a team and wagon could manage to make delivery.

Prosperity had arrived only to be snatched away when the Yellow Aster mine built its own mill. The big ore wagons no longer skidded down the steep Rand grade and lugged across

9

*The 5 stamp mill in the yard of the museum at Randsburg is out
of the old Red Dog mill.*

the sandy valley to the Garlock mills. Everything moved toward Rand Mountain where a rail line was coming in from San Bernardino, water was being piped from a spring to the east and there were mine jobs if one did not work his own claim. Men, business and buildings moved to Randsburg.

Johannesburg, a planned town just around the mountain from Randsburg, had its mills, stores, and saloons and boasted about its orderly growth compared to the haphazard Rand Camp. Its golf course, 9 holes played around the boundary of the town, was a rare desert refinement that lent prestige to the community. Lively rivalry between Johannesburg and Randsburg existed for years and was probably sparked by the fact that the Randsburg Railroad stopped at Johannesburg and never did get around the mountain to the larger town.

Long before gold was discovered in the Rand Mountains, Red Rock Canyon to the west had become a route south for explorers and the remnant of '49ers that had survived Death Valley. By the late 1860's deep, worn ruts had developed. Wagons, heavy with bullion from the Cerro Gordo silver mine, were churning the deep sand and leaving dust trails between the wind-and-water-sculptured walls of the canyon. Lone miners working the side washes waved at the passing drivers or came out to hear the latest news. An occasional big nugget teased the miners into staying and had the outside world watching for a new bonanza to develop.

Colorful as the canyon, was an emigrant who pedalled his bicycle through the valley enroute to the Panamint mines. Seeing the need for a rest stop for travelers, Koehn gave up his plans to reach the mines and built a way-station near a spring in view of Red Rock's red-and-pink-topped cliffs. When gold was discovered in Goler, Koehn was one of the first to arrive and brought a wagon load of supplies including stock for the first bar.

11

Koehn started a delivery route as mines increased and his wagon with food, dynamite, picks, shovels and mail was a welcome sight around Goler, Summit and the diggings all over Rand Mountain. His way-station became a favored stage stop where news of the mines was as recent as the delivery wagon's last trip.

When a big mining boom is over most associated communities fade away. Randsburg and Johannesburg were no exceptions. Men left for better pay, families moved away, and buildings became empty; signs of the end chilled the mountain communities. Then a new lease on life came in the form of a tungsten discovery in 1905. At first there was only rumor, then a railroad siding and finally men were being hired. Rand area was off on another bonanza that lasted until the demands of World War I were met. The price dropped and the mines closed.

The outlook was bleak. Very little gold was being processed and tungsten was finished. That hundreds of miners had been walking over high grade silver for years, came as a surprise in 1919 when two prospectors recognized the metal. A whole new show went into production about halfway between the Randsburg-Johannesburg gold fields and Atolia's tungsten.

Empty buildings became desirable property and movers went to work. Every usable structure was transported to a site near the new find and still the surge of miners outstripped the available housing. Miners and their families made do with tents, houses still on moving blocks, and shacks thrown together out of junk materials.

Two communities developed within a few rods of each other. One was Osdick named for a miner who held claims at the site and the other was known by a number of names including Inn City and Sin City. Postal department problems ended only after they disregarded the names heaped upon the two feuding communities and they designated the post office as Red Mountain.

There was local resentment over the postal department's decision, but by any name it was a wild place.

Red Mountain became well known as a wide open town where one could get a drink in any place of business except the post office. The Madams were proud of their high class houses, and the girls were most attractive. Prohibition had little effect as warnings came ahead of the raids, and the town turned temporarily dry. Shootings were hushed up and soon forgotten. Week nights the town was lively, but on Saturday night the place roared, bands came from Los Angeles to play through the night and out of town crowds arrived to join in the fun or watch the show. Long after the silver boom was over, Red Mountain lived on as an old-west type night spot.

There is only limited mining activity these days but old timers continue to look for a new boom and at times their hopes have been fanned by rumors. There was the year government men combed the old tunnels of the Yellow Aster to see if it would be suitable for storing valuable documents. It would have been a multi-million dollar deal, a boost to the community, and jobs for men. The tunnels were too deteriorated to reclaim. There was a rumor later that revolved around Randsburg becoming a tourist attraction with luxury swimming pools, motels, ore train trips and "packaged recreation" in an old mining town atmosphere.

The next rumor may turn into the real thing and the slumbering camps will spring to life. Now, before the next boom changes the face of things is an ideal time to become acquainted with the Rand. It is easy to reach from either highway 395 or 14. Visitors will need to have their own sleeping accommodations or plan to stay overnight in modern facilities at Four-Corners, Ridgecrest, Trona or Mojave, an approximately thirty mile drive to any one of them.

For supplies and souvenirs there is a general store and fountain, two bars, two antique stores, two bottle shops, an art gallery, and museum in Randsburg. Johannesburg has two filling stations, a cafe, and bottle shop. Red Mountain has a bottle shop and a filling station; there is no business place in Atolia, Garlock, Goler or Cantil.

Comfortable exploring of the desert, back roads and mining communities is best confined to three seasons. Spring is beautiful with flowers of multi-color and the air carries their light perfume of subtle mixtures. Fall is gold, tan and mauve against moving clouds. Winter, a time of varied moods, can quickly change from warm to cold, sunny to cloudy, and dark comes early in the canyons. Summers are hot, and not the time to explore back country or climb mountains.

There is something for almost everyone to enjoy in the Rand area. Without leaving hard surfaced roads there are ghost towns, abandoned mine camps, ranch country and a county museum that tells the mine story. Dirt roads, passable for passenger cars offer old landmarks that were the road signs for pioneers, gold diggings where one can pan out some "colors" the early miners passed up in their rush to greater riches, and scattered small camps where relics and bottles may be found. There is a safe tunnel that goes through a mountain, scenic canyons, Indian camp sites and modern ranching projects to visit. Beyond passenger car limits are freighter trails, mines, remains of Chinese camps and diggings, and virtually untouched rock, bottle and relic collecting.

Everywhere there is color—line and form to challenge the artist and photographer. History devotees have freight and borax routes to map, long forgotten way stations to locate, and ruins to identify. Railroad buffs can hike the old shoo-fly used when Southern Pacific built north to meet the Carson and Colorado's narrow gage. Only the road bed of the Randsburg Railroad is left, and one water tank still stands along the "Jackrabbit" line out of Mojave.

14

Plant and wild life is abundant in spite of the popular belief that the desert is without life. Rare plants exist in this region where an arid Death Valley band blends into an increasingly moist belt to the west. Animals, birds, reptiles and rodents make their year 'round home here, but seldom appear for public viewing; therein lies their survival.

Take a day, a week, a life time, and poke around the old diggings. Pan some gold, collect the beauty in rock or on film, discover the flowers that grow close to the ground with blooms no larger than a pin head, inhale the aroma of sage and greasewood after a desert shower. With eyes and mind join the raven as he glides on the air waves, free, relaxed and in tune with the desert world.

There is so much to experience in the Rand area that it reminds one of an old miners story about a traveling preacher. Word was sent ahead to announce a preaching date at a point half way between Summit and Goler diggings. Either the word didn't get around or the miners were too busy for no one showed up.

The preacher was about to give up waiting when he was delighted to see a lone prospector and burro coming along the narrow trail. After welcoming the ragged, bearded man the preacher went right into his sermon, which went on and on. The burro's ears drooped and the prospector sagged in his tracks. Finally the preacher paused and asked, "Now how was that for a sermon?"

The old prospector slowly adjusted the burro's pack, then turned to the preacher, "If I had a whole load of hay, I'd feed my burro some. I wouldn't give him the whole load at one time!"

This guide book is just a taste of what the Rand area has to offer. If you want the whole load there are volumes to read, old records to search and miles to explore after you have made an acquaintance with this fascinating bit of California.

15

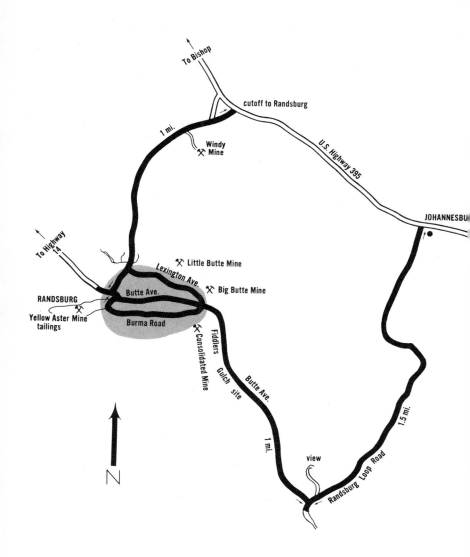

To Bishop

cutoff to Randsburg

1 mi.

Windy
Mine

U.S. Highway 395

JOHANNESBU

To Highway
14

Little Butte Mine

Lexington Ave.

Big Butte Mine

RANDSBURG

Butte Ave.

Yellow Aster Mine
tailings

Burma Road

Fiddlers
Gulch
site

Consolidated Mine

Butte Ave.

1 mi.

1.5 mi.

view

Randsburg Loop Road

N

**RANDSBURG**

# I. RANDSBURG

*A visit to this old gold camp that produced millionaires can be made by any type vehicle and year around; summer heat is not prohibitive at the altitude of 3500 feet.*

---

Want to stroll across a secret tunnel, examine the bullet holes left from a saloon brawl, stand at a bank window where gold headed the deposit slip, have an old-fashioned soda at an authentic old fountain or hike the picturesque eroded tailings of one of southern California's richest mines? Get in the mood by mentally stepping back to the time when three men discovered gold on the side of an unnamed mountain in the Mojave Desert.

It was the spring of 1895 and they let no one know of their discovery as they hurried to lay out claims, but by the time the first corners were marked prospectors started pouring in from every direction to stake claims for themselves. The nearest gold diggings were about ten miles away, yet the feel or knowledge of a new strike spread to even more distant camps. For want of an explanation old timers credited the phenomenon to the "sagebrush telegraph"; just how the news spread through the sparsely settled miles remains one of the desert's closely guarded secrets.

Rand Camp, like most early day mining camps of the west started as a sprawling tent community. Living conditions were rough and a miner was considered fortunate to have a tent, a wagon box or even a tarp to drape over bushes for a shelter. Wind vigorously worked at adding to man's discomfort. Summer heat had a way of bearing down and sapping moisture while freezing temperatures reinforced with an occasional snow was often winter fare. It was no place for the timid or weak.

Similar to other thriving mine camps, one of the first business places was a tent saloon furnished with a plank bar and a few makeshift card tables on the side. The tables relieved the miner from the burden of carrying his heavy gold around with him and the bar provided fuel to fire him up for another go at the hard work of mining.

As Rand gold lived up to and exceeded the rumors, the camp boomed into a town of many businesses including hotels, saloons, stores and a theatre. There was an atmosphere, a community personality unique to Randsburg, some of which is still there for the discerning visitor to experience.

The remains of the fascinating old camp can be reached from either Highway 395 or 14 via hard surfaced roads that converge at the edge of town and swing into Butte Avenue. First impression is that of a movie or T.V. set using false front buildings. These are not make believe; they are real and their life story reaches far back before the flicks or the tube.

The post office, easily identifiable on the right side of the street is an ideal point from which to start exploring. Take a look at the post office itself before moving on. The thick adobe walls were built as protection against the many disastrous fires that hit the dry camp before the turn of the century. The walls stood through the holocausts but the roof was replaced a number of times. The building had many lives, both good and not so good before gaining respectability in its present service to the community. In spite of its small size the building served for a number of years as a rooming house where the beds never got cold; when one miner went to work another came in to sleep. There were three shifts at the mine and three shifts to each bed.

On one side of the post office is an old building that served as Union headquarters for the battle waged by the miner's union in their effort to organize the Yellow Aster Mine on the hill above

18

town. That was a period of near disaster for the mine; fires were set in the tunnels, fights erupting and men were out of work. It was a time when there were two Saturday night dances, one union, one nonunion. Union men were not allowed to dance with a girl that had been at the nonunion dance, but women were in short supply and there was active stealing of girls from one dance to the other.

On the other side of the post office is the general store which stocks everything from patent medicines to miner's lights and gold pans just as it did back in boom times. Toward the back of the store is a soda fountain where years ago the famous ice cream creation "The Gondola" was born and the miner's after-work drink, "Salty Joe." Visitors today, served at the same fountain can enjoy old-fashioned cold drinks and thick sodas while studying the true to life action in an oil painting hanging over the mirrored back bar.

Though the old White House Saloon across the street no longer serves Flusseys (three shots of whiskey) for twenty-five cents, it is a most interesting place to visit. The street entrance opens into a large room filled with displays of antiques and often the visitor can watch the husband and wife team creating original gold and silver jewelry. Visit the dimly lighted bar room off to the side. Stand at the now silent, empty bar and listen well. There could be the faint tinkle of glass, the soft laughter of the girls, the muffled slap of cards, and the stomp of miners' heavy boots silenced by the whine of bullets.

The massive bar was built by Yellow Aster carpenters, bullet holes in the walls attest to disagreements among the customers and the old cash register knew well the story of miners separated from their hard earned gold. Not on display but still in working order is a huge dumb-waiter that carried food orders from the restaurant in the basement to the bar patrons. Below street level

19

*Winter brings occasional snow that completely changes the Randsburg scene.*

20

was not only a busy restaurant, but an ice house and wine cellar that supplied the other businesses in town. Along the stairway from the street to the restaurant was a door that has long been boarded up. Beyond the door was a tunnel heading up the hill toward the Yellow Aster Mine and its gold. It is believed some highgrading went on through this tunnel but it was known best as a sanctuary for individuals hiding from the law.

The roof above the bar was recessed, a place for the girls to entertain gentlemen on nights when it was too warm for comfort inside the buildings. Back of the old White House, on the next street level down, are a few shacks left over from the extensive red light district that was a part of the struggling young mine camp. The girls added a touch of refinement to an almost totally male population. Laughter, love, discouragement and death like the old tunes played on the piano in the corner, were real life episodes played within the walls of thirty some saloons up and down the long street. Randsburg wasn't as bad as some mine camps are reported to have been, but it was far from a dull place. The metal shutters, still in place on the front and sides of the White House were not for looks. They were installed as insurance against stray bullets hitting a patron when street fights were common.

Though the fancy dressed girls and the four-a-day stage coaches arriving in a cloud of dust are gone, there is still a lot of gold mining going on in the one remaining bar. Old timers used to say that more and bigger gold was dug along the bar of a saloon than ever saw the light of day at the end of a pick and shovel.

On up Butte Avenue are bottle and relic shops where the discards of yesterday become the treasure of today. Variety is in evidence on every shelf and information on age or former contents are free for the asking.

A picnic-rest area next to the museum is a pleasant spot to

*Randsburg today as seen from the high hill just off the Loop road between Randsburg and Johannesburg.*

pause, relax and view the buildings lining the long street. Study the equipment, mine locomotive, working parts of a stamp mill and other artifacts rescued from abandoned mines. The first thing that the visitor sees upon entering the museum, which is open weekends, is a unique dinner of rocks that are so realistic in shape and color that they appear eatable.

An old barber shop and gas station next door to the museum have been converted to an art gallery, but the exteriors have remained the same. Farther up the street, on the opposite side is an imposing building that housed the Randsburg Bank, a general store and a furniture store. The bank is open weekends for the interest and enjoyment of visitors. The store is being stocked with old furniture and other items while machinery accumulates along the front of the building.

Near the Catholic Church, turn right up Burma Road. The building cornering on Butte and Burma Roads was Randsburg's first printing office. On the left of the first curve is a small house with gingerbread trim; it was the camp's first school building. Burma Road, an oil surfaced street, climbs to an area that has few dwellings compared to the old days, but gives a good view of the present community, which is only a ghost of the original robust mining camp.

A badly eroded oil topped road cuts off to the left as Burma Road starts back down to Butte Avenue. This was the entrance route to the Yellow Aster Mine and along it were the homes of the mine owners and the company office. Fire, wind and the years have taken a toll; the office building is collapsing and only one home remains livable. The road is rough, there is no turning around point and the gate to the mine is locked. The mine itself is not open to visitors as the tunnels that honey-comb the place are caving, the old mill building is a twisted burned mass, and the glory hole no longer has any glory.

23

Upon returning to Butte Avenue go left a few feet and then right, past the abandoned jail and before crossing the bridge go right on Lexington. This street is lined with homes that housed the early mining families. Exteriors have changed little but a majority have modern, comfortable interiors with interesting room combinations and split levels where cabins were moved together to form a house.

Across the wash from this residential area can be seen the weathered, picturesque skeleton of the Little Butte Mine buildings. When Lexington enters Butte Avenue, turn left. The big mine operation on the hill straight ahead is the Big Butte Mine and Mill. This mill continued in operation until a few years ago, one of the last, if not the last gold mill in California. Before it shut down it was processing ore from California's southernmost border to its north, also from Nevada, and Arizona to the east. For years the price of gold remained the same but the operating costs rose for both the mill and the miners until the shut down was inevitable.

View the Big Butte from the road; it is not a place to explore without a guide. Like most old mines, the shaft is deep and dangerous, shoring and ladders are no longer safe, and cyanide, a poison to be avoided, used in the milling process is everywhere.

Follow Butte Avenue around the bend on the way out of town and you are in Fiddler's Gulch. In 1896 this narrow wash was a lively place populated with men living in tents and dugouts. What went on here was strictly their business and the elite of Rand Camp kept a strict hands-off policy. By day the men worked at the Yellow Aster or right in the gulch. The Big Dyke, California Mine, Maria, Dos Picannini, Hard Cash and the Miner's Dream kept a good many of the men working where they lived. At night the gulch hummed with another kind of activity. The sounds of merry-making mixed with homespun music bounced from moun-

24

tain side to mountain side with now and then a pistol shot to liven things up.

A few wind scarred and sun baked old head frames still stand over shafts that for years have had no sounds of men at work, underground blasts, or loaded ore buckets being brought to the surface. The dugouts have slowly disappeared leaving only one here and there to testify to Fiddler's Gulch occupancy. Even the wind singing through the old timbers and swaying the lacy limbs of greasewood does little now to stir up a vision of what the gulch was like some seventy years ago.

A mile out of Randsburg a white post indicates Loop Road to the left. Within a few feet a dirt trail takes off to the left and makes a steep climb a half mile to the mountain top. This side road is not for passenger cars but the hike to the crest is worth the exercise. The birdseye view takes in Randsburg on one side and Johannesburg on the other; distant mountains seem so close and Telescope Peak, in Death Valley, stands out sharp and beautiful.

Continue on the hard surfaced Loop Road, dropping down into Johannesburg and onto Highway 395. Turn left at the highway and within a mile the cutoff to Randsburg means another left branch. Up on the mountain, silhouetted against the sky, is the Windy Mine; the name is appropriate for there is plenty of wind day after day, except down in the mine.

For bottle collectors the right side of the road has been good hunting ground. For years the town dump was any convenient place over the side of a hill or canyon, not always out of sight. One might liken it to a garden of tin and glass planted by careless early residents, that is now being harvested by relic collectors, deplored by the ecology minded, and ignored by the local citizens.

Like the secret tunnel crossing the main street and the tin strewn mountain side, other remnants of the gold boom days wait to be discovered by those who have time to explore.

25

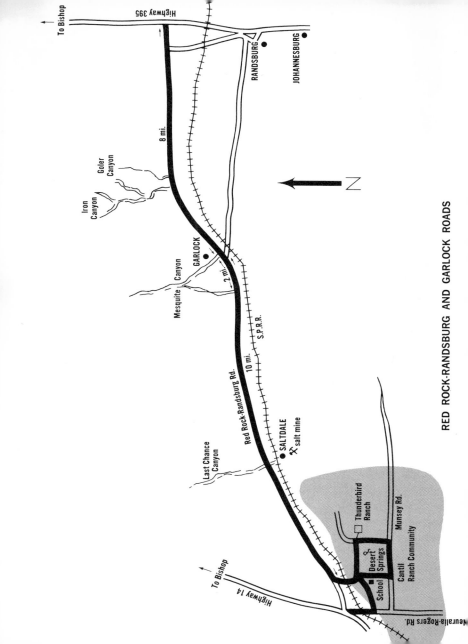

RED ROCK-RANDSBURG AND GARLOCK ROADS

# 2. RED ROCK-RANDSBURG AND GARLOCK ROADS

*The cool days between October and mid June are best for explor-
ing along the southeast slope of the El Paso Range. This trip is a
link between Highway 14 and 395, offering variety from ghost
towns to rare horses.*

---

Angling north out of Mojave, Highway 14 goes through twenty
miles of desert vegetation that has adapted to limited moisture
and extreme temperatures. Joshuas, aged monarchs of this land,
tower above the other growth while the fragile appearing greasewood gives a lacy soft contrast to the other stiff, thorny plants.
Twice a year the highway is bordered by a wide strip of flowering
gold. Coreopsis and desert dandelion predominate in spring; rab-
bitbrush and yellowhead carry the fall banner.

Green alfalfa fields unexpectedly appear to the right near the
point of departure from Highway 14. On a slight curve at a sprawling old building with the fading name "Wagon Wheel," branch
sharp right on hard surfaced Neuralia Road. Continue south about
a mile, cross railroad tracks, and turn left to Cantil. Like many
small desert communities that were indispensable back in the
horse and buggy days, Cantil has lost its importance through
modern transportation. Today the railroad shipping corrals are
empty, trucks go direct to the ranches to load.

There remains a siding from which clay is shipped. If one hap-
pens to be in Cantil as a freight car is being loaded it is an interesting process to watch as the ancient truck backs up the old
ramp, hangs over the freight car and slowly drops its load. There
are times when local betting gets rather exciting over whether the
skilled driver will keep the truck on the ramp or go an inch too
far and flip the whole thing into the freight car. The material

27

*Granny Slocum's sagging old house framed by the doorway of a ruin along the road in Garlock.*

loaded here comes from one of the few known sources in the world of pure white clay used by fine china makers.

Though the little freight-depot building and section men's homes are gone, the water tank, one of very few left in California, stands as a monument to an era when the steam locomotive needed a drink every few miles. Southern Pacific's Jawbone Division reached Cantil in 1908 with a crew of four hundred men and nine hundred horses pushing the rails on north to connect with the Carson and Colorado in Owen's Valley. The coaches were hot in summer, cold in winter, but offered the passengers an exciting ride. Fights were frequent between the varied nationalities traveling to jobs on the construction of the Los Angeles aqueduct. "Harmless" little games set up by professional gamblers, or pleasant conversation with girls on their way to the mine camps, helped to pass the time.

Cantil's small country store is now an empty building with vacant windows. The post office, long the focal point of this ranch country, has moved up onto the highway leaving only the school and the assayer. Martin Engel, last of the fire assayers, came to the area in the 1920's, prospecting, mining and assaying material from all over the area being explored through this book. Fortunate is the visitor to Cantil who stops to make Engel's acquaintance and watch the age old method of analysing ore samples.

For the assayer the process is one of absolute accuracy in the use of chemicals, heat and weight. For the prospector the assayer's statement is like receiving a school report card showing how well the prospector knew his geology and rock formations.

From Engel's assay building and the abandoned store turn south on Norton Road, past the school and into ranch country. For over fifty years men have waged a battle here against the desert. There were times when modern technology seemed to be winning but wind driven sand like military reinforcements would rush in to cut off, tear up, or bury plants, fences and buildings. The war between man and nature started over time after time until slowly, acre by acre the desert is being converted to alfalfa fields and pasture.

On the opposite side of the road from the school, is the Burch Ranch where the young owner manages to mix ranching and restoring antique cars. Visitors interested in old cars or modern ranching methods are welcome.

Norton Road ends against the border of a large sheep and alfalfa spread. Turn left on Munsey Road; the dilapidated buildings in a field to the left are the remains of the Munsey Ranch, one of the early day, "hard scrabble" efforts to outwit the desert. Within a mile turn left on Pappas Road. Munsey continues on east but runs out of solid surfacing and fades into an old freight trail that is not for passenger cars.

Just over a mile on Pappas Road a sign and a dirt road to the left indicate Desert Springs, one of California's lesser publicized but important historic spots. If there are indications of recent rains, walk the short distance into the monument. It becomes a bit spongy around the spring in damp weather and to walk where famous persons once trod can add meaning to the visit.

Desert Springs was well known to the Indians long before 1834 when Joseph Walker first found the life-saving water. Ten years later John C. Fremont camped at the spring and lent his name to the valley. The Jayhawker party that survived Death Valley in 1849 were led to this spring after walking days without water. In later years the spring became a well known rest stop on freight and stage routes. Harry Ball's Way-station, near the spring, added notoriety by building a reputation of watered liquor, tough meat and half cooked beans.

Desert Springs like many other natural water sources along the foothills of the El Paso Range is now only a miniature of what it

30

was a hundred years ago. Trees that gave a wide shade area, native grass that fed horses and cattle and the marsh land about the spring are nearly gone. Deep wells, irrigation of hundreds of acres of alfalfa and heavy domestic use may in part be responsible for the change.

Just beyond Desert Springs to the right of the road is Thunderbird Ranch where the rare Peruvian Paso horse is raised. Visitors are welcome to view these beautiful and unusual animals of which there are only about two hundred in the U.S. The Thunderbird, top in show horses, is one of the largest Peruvian Paso breeders and trainers in North America.

The Peruvian Paso, born with five natural gaits (other breeds have to be trained to their gaits), is a breed developed from the best qualities of the two types of horses brought in to South America by the Conquistadores. Peruvian ranches, where wealth and status is measured by the Paso ownership, have been reluctant to let any of the stock leave their country, but the Thunderbird has managed to obtain top ranking show and breeding horses. Native Peruvian trainers live on the ranch using methods and riding gear from their home land.

From the ranch gate head west to a cross road near the old Cantil store building, turn right, crossing the railroad tracks and on out to Red Rock-Randsburg Road. Turn right into this well used short cut to one of the Death Valley routes. The present road is a little to the north of an old twenty mule team borax route but virtually follows the same course along the valley.

There may not be traffic as on a freeway, but parking in the road or leaving a door hanging open is a sure invitation to be hit by a freight truck or another visitor to the area. This may seem far from traffic and signal lights but only the signals are scarce.

Six miles from the point of entering Red Rock-Randsburg road a good trail drops toward a mill on the edge of Koehn Dry Lake

31

*Thunderbird Ranch has thoroughbred Peruvian Paso horses that are top award winners in Peru and the United States. Peruvian riding costume, riding gear and training can be seen at the ranch.*

where the American Salt Company processes salt for industrial use. No longer processed is a unique material found in the lake which proved ideal defogging for helicopters in Vietnam.

In summer this white expanse of salt crystals reflects the sun's rays producing temperatures that compete with Death Valley and evaporation is rapid. This particular condition made salt production seem feasible when the Diamond Salt Company built the first mill in 1911, almost entirely a hand operation. Cloth sacks were made on a home type sewing machine right in the mill building while men sawed chunks of salt out of the lake, loaded by hand into ore cars that were often pushed by hand until out on solid ground where a small engine could take over. After being ground the salt was packaged by hand and loaded in freight cars sack by sack.

Today a rich brine is pumped from below the lake, evaporative beds separate unwanted minerals from the salt and from there on modern processing speeds it to market with few men involved. There is no longer a need for the company town that was Saltdale.

Obviously there are hazards around the plant and the steep mounds of salt. If you wish to visit the plant, examine the beautiful crystals, watch the milling process or stand at the edge of the evaporative beds where the raspberry pink liquid with a white border reflects the El Paso Mountains, ask permission of the manager at the office in the mill building.

Continue on the Red Rock-Randsburg Road to a "Y" with highway signs indicating Randsburg to the east and left to the ruins of the old town of Garlock. Only a few structures and piles of rocks remain to mark the site of a once sizeable community that predates all other towns in the area. It started as an early day water and supply point for cattlemen and freighters hauling borax out and supplies back. Gold miners and gold mills came in the 1890's to boom the small settlement into a town of importance

33

with hotels, boarding houses, saloons, assayers, mine promoter offices, post office, Wells Fargo office and two to four stages a day.

The most pretentious building still standing is often mistaken for a bank, but was a saloon and bawdy house that probably handled more gold in a day than did the Wells Fargo office and the nearest bank. Main street crossed the present road and ran along the side of the saloon. A two story hotel, the elite of the 1890's, was the stage stop just opposite the saloon.

The walls of Jennie's Bar, that stood like a fortress for years, have succumbed to time and treasure hunters, and are now a heap of rock and adobe. An old Mexican-type arrastra, or drag mill stands a short distance from the historical marker. Though this one was mechanized, instead of operated by a burro, it does show how boulders were dragged around and around to pulverize ore and release the gold. North of the arrastra is what was used as a blacksmith shop after the railroad began discarding broken ties. Still farther north are the remains of an adobe home built in 1896.

The famous Garlock mill that processed the first gold from Randsburg's Yellow Aster Mine was close to the present railroad but at the time of the mill operation all hauling was still dependent on teams. The site can be located by a rock foundation and a deep well which is fenced for the protection of visitors. Six mills were in operation until 1906 when the Yellow Aster built its own mill. Buildings and families moved up the hill to Randsburg where the new mill had work for men.

Two and a half miles northeast, a good dirt road to the left goes up Iron Canyon where abandoned mines, a few cabins belonging to weekend residents and some new prospect holes add up to little of unusual interest to compensate for the drive. Hunters frequent the canyon in fall and gold prospectors avoiding the sand of Goler Wash come in this way and make a short hike down into the old Goler diggings.

Historic Goler Gulch, wash or canyon, by whatever term one

34

chooses is no longer an easy place to visit even for four wheel drive vehicles. Loose sand has grown deeper by the year, waiting to be cleared out by a flash flood as happened a few years ago. A couple of old cabins still stand along the bank but the famous gold diggings of the 1890's which ran for miles underground were filled and covered in the flood, even the drainage system changed, and the old landmarks are difficult to locate.

A short distance beyond the cluster of tamarisk trees and the remains of a water pumping station, are the ruins of a mill high on the bank to the left of the road. The ditch between the road and the mill site is the Garlock Fault which has been running along the Garlock Road and crossing it at some points but nowhere is it as easy to recognize as at this particular spot.

Three miles farther on there is a choice of going ahead one mile to Highway 395 or branching right on a road to Randsburg and the highway. For bottle collectors the road to Randsburg offers the old Teagle loading platform near where the road crossed the railroad tracks. A relatively untouched area to search, it could produce sun purpled liquor and medicine bottles as have been found at other freight stops and along the tracks.

In the valley ahead are leavings that were part of a gold dredge operation. The massive, rusting dredge was recently sold for scrap but where it operated is still much in evidence on the right side of the road. Here are the scars of a unique effort to form an artificial lake and float the dredge. Deep wells were put into operation to keep the lake filled but more water departed into the air and out through the sand in the bottom than stayed in the lake. Old time dry-wash miners had many good laughs at the expense of the metal monster that was so out of its element in the dry desert.

The road deadends at the top of the hill, to the left is Highway 395 or to the right the town of Randsburg, with its gold rich history and mine camp legends.

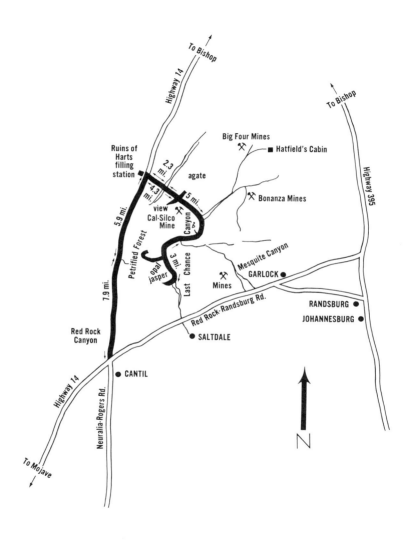

**LAST CHANCE CANYON**

# 3. LAST CHANCE CANYON

*Mid October to June is the time of year to experience this canyon of scenic beauty, geological caprice and human escapades, accessible to modern passenger cars as well as four wheel drive vehicles.*

---

The route into Last Chance Canyon that most frequently appears on maps and rockhound guides shows the road branching off Red Rock-Randsburg Road. Avoid it! Never an easy trail to travel, it now has deep washes to cross, parts of the road bed are gone and the narrow, blind curves are not improving.

Instead of turning east at the old Wagon Wheel Cafe junction, continue on Highway 14 heading north through Red Rock Canyon. Within eight miles a sign on the right announces, "Opal Mine" a privately owned development. For a nominal charge anyone can hunt for fire opal. Road conditions vary so it is advisable to inquire locally before attempting with a passenger car.

Approximately fourteen miles from the Wagon Wheel landmark (thirty-six miles north of Mojave), a good dirt road to the right leaves Highway 14 directly opposite the remains of Hart's filling station. This entrance to the canyon is well traveled and presents no problems as long as one stays on the road. The soft, sandy shoulders are not for driving or turning around. Fawn colored landscape stretches out for three miles interrupted only by an occasional dark green Joshua. A gem quality agate field is marked by the appearance of gray-white hills to the left. Some chunks of the material can be found by walking a short distance on either side of the road but for good collecting continue on for a mile until nearly opposite the hills. A fair road takes off to the

*Unusual formation of Feldspar appears like steps along the side of a granite wall.*

agate field but a better one for cars is nearly a mile farther on where an excellent dirt road crosses the main route. The left branch goes to a camping area within easy reach of the agate that appears in layers of mottled blue, pink, tan to deep carmel.

The road to the right, opposite the one going to the agate field, stops at the rim of the canyon where there is a splendid view of pumice mining and Last Chance Canyon's strawberry, chocolate, vanilla, ice cream sundae country.

Continuing on the main road, a windmill, water tanks and an extensive mining-milling operation comes into view. It was here in the early 1930's that a prospector, who managed to divert his eyes and thoughts from gold, found a sizeable ledge of pure white pumice or volcanic ash. The discovery developed into the home of the Holly Cleanser that became a competitor of the widely advertised Dutch Cleanser which was mining similar material a few miles to the south.

Presently owned by Calsilco, the operation is active when demand cuts down the stockpile. The mill produces material used in products that vary from insulation and acoustical plaster of the building trade, to oil absorbing filters, cleaning compounds and soil conditioner for golf courses. The very finest grade, that feels like silk, is used in tooth powder and polish for gold, silver, copper and chrome objects.

The road skirts left of the mill and tops a hill approximately five miles from Highway 14. An interesting side jaunt can be made by taking a sharp turn to the left onto a little-used trail that runs along the ridge of the hill for less than a mile. Stop as the road dips toward another valley opposite a little gray cabin off on another ridge to the right.

The route ahead leads into interesting country but the road frequently changes; one day it is excellent and the next day after a rain it will be a jumble of boulders. Walk the steep grade before

*Chinese miners relaxed with their pipe, a bit of gambling or a few drinks in this dugout.*

attempting with a car, keeping in mind that this is the only way out unless you have a four wheel drive vehicle.

The explorer who has to turn around at this point need not go away disappointed. Scoop up a handful of the black sand at the bottom of the two tracks cut by years of travel, or get down on your knees; in either case blow gently to separate and move the black sand. Chances are there will be flakes of gold showing where the sand had been. Known as flour gold, it is so fine that a slight breeze will carry it away.

Walk along the edge of the hill to the right of the road and look down at the numerous gold diggings that dot the side of the mountain where miners followed an ancient stream bed. The gold was cemented to or deposited between the boulders that now lie strewn about the mouth of the eighty or ninety year old mines. Some of the tunnels are a mile long, twisting and turning into the mountain. None of them are safe to explore for they have not been worked for years, the walls are crumbling, old timbers are rotted, and boulders hang ready to fall.

This area was known as Upper Bonanza Gulch by early day miners and the scar of one of the richest diggings can be seen across the valley. That operation clung to the steep side of a cliff; below it in a narrow wash are dugouts where miners lived who worked their own claims. The holes can not be seen from this point but they can be reached by a good road once you are in the valley.

From the stories told by the miners these holes used as living quarters were dug and first occupied by Caucasian miners who left when they thought all the gold was worked out. A number of Chinese moved in to work the skimpy leavings and they too lived in the dugouts. One in particular on the west bank was supposedly an opium den. The Orientals kept to themselves, bothering no one and no one bothered them—that is until word got around

*Pumice for Dutch Cleanser came from ledge of white, top left. Track for ore cars bringing material to valley floor is the long sweeping line down through center of picture.*

that their tunneling under the floor of the wash was producing plenty of gold.

The Chinese, of small stature, dug only narrow passages, just large enough to crawl in and move a short handled shovel. These miniature tunnels were useless to the white miners who talked of repossessing the wash. Rumor did seep out that the Chinese tunnels were blasted shut while the men were at work but there was no factual report as to why there were no more Chinese seen around Bonanza Gulch. In recent years prospectors have broken into small tunnels and unearthed human bones, short handled picks and shovels.

Far to the left of the valley are other mines and an occasional building. One cabin clinging to the mountain side was the temporary home of Hatfield the rain maker. Hatfield built a dam below the cabin on a natural runoff system from Black Mountain, the predominating earthen mass to the east. Theoretically, a big rain would carry gold down from the mountain and deposit it against the dam from which it could be easily collected. Hatfield started the rain, and as in other places he couldn't turn it off at the right time. The dam broke and water, gold, along with Hatfield's dream, tumbled down into Bonanza Gulch where nuggets are still found; the last one reported was January of 1973.

Return to the main road after the Bonanza Gulch side trip and turn left taking the western-most branch of two routes paralleling each other. There is a gradual descent for the next mile which levels off in the main channel of Last Chance Canyon. This is scenic backcountry, an area favored by campers, explorers, rock collectors and photographers. There is a surprising amount of traffic, especially on weekends and road courtesy is essential. Pull off onto solid, level areas so the other fellow can pass without having to drive onto a sandy shoulder; the big campers and travel trailers especially need consideration.

43

At the "T" on the valley floor take the road to the right (the left branch is part of trip #10). Eight miles from where you left Highway 14, is an emergency source of water. Lee Springs, approximately one-quarter-mile off the main road can be reached by making a sharp right hand curve into a sandy path that skirts around a low hill to a rock house and the spring.

The main road meanders along a dry creek bed between cliffs of bone-colored silica that through the ages have been sculptured into geological grandeur. Here is a chapter of earth's history telling of ancient volcanic explosions that laid down a great mantle of white silica and then capped the whole thing with a lava flow. Later the mountain range lifted toward the south and sank to the north. Erosion set to work on the soft silica, undermining and carrying it away until the rhyolite cap collapsed in jumbled masses, jagged crags, and steep cliffs, exposing islands of varied color that give the canyon its unique beauty. This is nature's studio where line, color and design is exhibited on a gigantic scale.

Two miles from the point of entering the canyon, there is an unusual formation of feldspar appearing like steps on a flat granite wall. The road curves around the granite to a camp area below a natural bridge. A dozen or more vehicles can be accommodated in this picturesque, sheltered area, where sounds echo against the mountain side and at night the stars are almost too large and bright to be real.

Seven tenths of a mile beyond the camp area there are dual roads. Turn to the right off of either of them to reach white eroded cliffs where a petrified forest once stood. The standing trees, stumps and logs have gone home with collectors but there are still twigs, roots and sizeable slivers of blue to brown agatized wood to be found. As the silica erodes away, new pieces are exposed.

There are level parking and camping spots near the beautiful cliffs. Old paths that wound through the forest are still fun to explore as they go over and around humps of silica. For color photography, early morning and toward evening are best. The fantastic erosion patterns in the white cliffs become nothing in the glare of mid-day sunlight. Because of the intense reflection here, this is definitely no place to be on a hot summer day!

Rejoining the main road after the petrified forest side trip, there is a steep mountain a short distance ahead that forces the path to go either right or left. The mountain has extensive gold diggings along a ledge that can be seen from the road. Known as Grubstake Hill, it was worked by men who needed enough gold to replenish their supplies so they could go elsewhere to dig gold. The matrix holding the gold was so difficult to remove from the precious metal that it was mined only as a last resort.

This is a good place to turn around or go to the right. The left arm of the road becomes too rough for passenger cars. Part of the old road is gone, boulders block the way and the side walls come in too close for comfort. If you have time, a hike of a quarter-mile will bring you to the old Cudahay, "Dutch Cleanser" camp site. The pumice processed here came from a ridge above the petrified forest.

The short road to the right dead ends at a camp area with a dry falls to climb for fire opal, milk opal and jasper. There are usually rockhounds camped here, sharing their knowledge and examining each other's discovery of the day.

The return trip to Highway 14, back tracking, will be all new. The view from this direction, the change in lighting, color and angle of the formations gives double value in spectacular scenery. It is a canyon that beckons you back time and time again, and each visit will reveal additional beauty that changes with the time of day, the season and your own awareness.

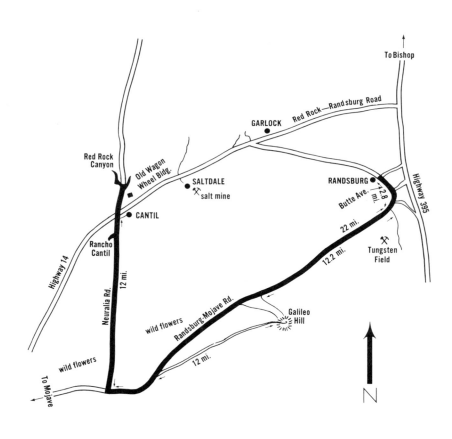

**RED ROCK CANYON, NEURALIA ROAD, AND RANDSBURG-MOJAVE ROAD**

# 4. RED ROCK CANYON, NEURALIA ROAD, AND RANDSBURG-MOJAVE ROAD

*From a land of fantasy that grips the imagination to miles of peaceful solitude, this is an area to visit during the cool months between October and June.*

Travelers on Highway 14, heading north from Mojave, cut through Red Rock Canyon and have only a mini look at a few colorful cliffs before the road returns to stretches of sand, sage, mesquite and joshua. The limited view from a speeding car isn't even a sample of what can be enjoyed by taking a few of the side roads. Behind the cliffs, around a corner or over a hump is unique beauty in color, and shape. The good dirt trails are short exploratory trips to exceptional views, and eroded formations.

Through the years, visitors have in imagination seen all types of things in this studio of nature's sculpture, and given them names. There is Cathedral City, the White House Cliffs, Buried City, Heliopolis Temple of the Sun, Tai Shan Temple and such mundane things as Camel Rocks and Elephant Head. Much of Red Rock's back country has appeared in movie and T.V. shows and they have called the formations hideouts, outlaw country, spy headquarters; no two people see the same thing in this wonderland.

Find a high spot and gaze down upon this enigma of color, cliffs, valleys and roads where a hundred years ago only a wagon trail wound in and out of the boulders in the main wash. Early travelers, except for Remi Nadeau's teams, were few in those days. Silver from Cerro Gordo, Owens Lake country, was hauled

47

*Openings to mine tunnels, dynamite storage caves and propect test holes pockmark the desert as Randsburg-Mojave Road nears Highway 395.*

over this route to the Los Angeles market. Some place in Red Rock Canyon was a way station where there was food for men and animals, a place to change teams, rest and exchange the latest news from north and south.

The canyon was beautiful then as now but many of those early day freighters left the impression that they dreaded the drive through the deep sand that pulled at the wagon wheels until the horses and mules were unable to keep the load moving. The load south was only one layer of silver ingots on the wagon bed but they were heavy; the return trip carried hay stacked high and a perfect wind catcher.

Wind and sand were bad enough but rain was the real threat. Beautiful thunderheads along the canyon rim was a warning that no time should be lost in getting out to the open desert. Flash floods moved everything in their path tumbling boulders, wagons, teams and drivers. One driver lived to tell of his jump from the wagon and desperate scramble up a hill side. The load of silver, wagon and team was buried somewhere under tons of debris. Fifty years later a silver ingot found in the canyon was believed to have been from this incident.

The canyon has much to offer any visitor and for treasure hunters there is at least one load of silver bullion still buried in the canyon or along one of its drainage channels. The photographer and artist will find another type of treasure in the elusive beauty that challenges man and modern techniques. The railroad buff can trace out the Red Rock Railroad line that was washed out by a flash flood that left rails twisted like pretzels.

Contrast, the test of any adventure lies not only in the canyon but along the roads radiating out and beyond its pageant of grandeur. Approximately five miles south of Red Rock Canyon where Highway 14 swings west, take Neuralia Road south. After crossing the railroad track a cluster of houses on the right is an

49

*Visitors are welcome at Rancho Cantil, home of thoroughbred horses and the new breed Cantil Pony which was developed for youthful riders. There is also room for a couple of "desert songbirds" of unknown ancestors.*

example of present day determination to carve out a home in the desert. The small settlement is Rancho Seco, built by a group of retirees and weekenders, that have fought wind, sand and flood while bringing their plans into reality.

About four miles farther, on the same side of the road is the gate to Rancho Cantil, home of the Cantil Pony. Visitors are welcome to watch the ponies being trained or see thoroughbred stallions, Arabian to Shetland pony, being exercised. The woman who owns and operates the ranch dreamed of developing a new breed of horse to meet the need of young riders. Years of breeding went into the Cantil Pony which is just the right height for the youth who is too old for a pony, yet too small to handle the full sized horse.

Neuralia Road leaves the ranch country and cuts through desert that can be on the move when the wind is at work, a shimmering sea of heat waves in summer or a garden of wildflowers in spring. Like a carpet of green and purple, acres of Persian Prince or Thistle Sage spread out to a lavender haze in the distance. A close examination of the plant that stands approximately two feet high reveals one of the desert's most fascinating wild flowers. A series of flower clusters like pale green balls of wool encircled with lacy orchid blooms are supported on a stout purplish stem covered with white wool. Acres of these unusual flowers stand above the less conspicuous Frost Mat, a rosette of minute green leaves and white flowers that hug the ground. A few poppies, and other blooms of gold add an interesting color contrast.

When Neuralia Road enters California City, turn left on Randsburg-Mojave Road. This is a place to replenish supplies and check the gas tank; the next filling station is twenty-five miles away. Since weekends are busy in this relatively new desert community there may be a free barbecue in process, an art show or no telling what has been scheduled as a public attraction.

52

Stay on Randsburg-Mojave Road one and a half miles then at a "Y" keep to the left as it becomes a good graded dirt road. Ahead are the great open spaces along a route traveled seventy-five years ago by ore wagons, stage coaches and spring wagons used by individuals hauling their gold to Mojave, meeting the train or replenishing supplies or on their way out to "civilization." Those early travelers had little choice of vehicle or weather conditions; today the trip is made in comfort, and visitors can select the time of year.

Spring is the most ideal time to drive this old wagon road that encourages frequent stops just for viewing the land, and inhaling the pot-pourri fragrance of wild flowers. It is an easy place to relax for the sight of gently swaying plants that send ripples of yellow, white and lavender toward the distant horizon have a hypnotic effect that shuts out a frenzied world. The display varies from year to year depending on rainfall and temperatures but from early March to mid-May chances are good that fiddleneck, desert candle, poppy, coreopsis, gilias, yellow saucers, blazing stars and many others will greet the visitor.

A large sign on the right indicates a side trip to Galileo Hill where a maintained road winds up to a peak that offers a spectacular view of the surrounding desert. Ancient roads, new roads, and miles of desert are seen as if from a plane. The San Bernardino Mountains, on one side and the Sierras on the other seem so close, even Telescope Peak of Death Valley, over one hundred and fifty miles away shows its snow covered peak against dark blue sky.

Randsburg-Mojave Road continues through a wide flat valley that, in spring, is the feeding grounds of large flocks of sheep. The sight and sound of hundreds of ewes and their lambs conversing and eating while a lone man and his dog guide and guard is a scene of pastoral life similar to that in many European coun-

53

*In spring flocks of sheep graze the desert as a lone Basque herder and his dog guide and guard them.*

tries. The herder, a Basque, was raised in a land between Spain and France where his skills were learned as a small boy, alone on a mountain side, watching the family flock.

Characteristic of the desert are miles that show little of man's scars but suddenly deep gouges and old buildings indicate his handiwork. Heaps of mine tailings announce a tungsten field that boomed and then died when World War I needs were over.

Good dirt roads like the arms of an octopus reach out to Highway 395 and Randsburg. To the left of this point of departure from Randsburg-Mojave Road there is a cluster of old mine structures, tailings and houses known as "Dog Patch." Why such a name? Who knows. Many different versions have been given and all of them or none may have some basis of truth. That too is characteristic of desert country.

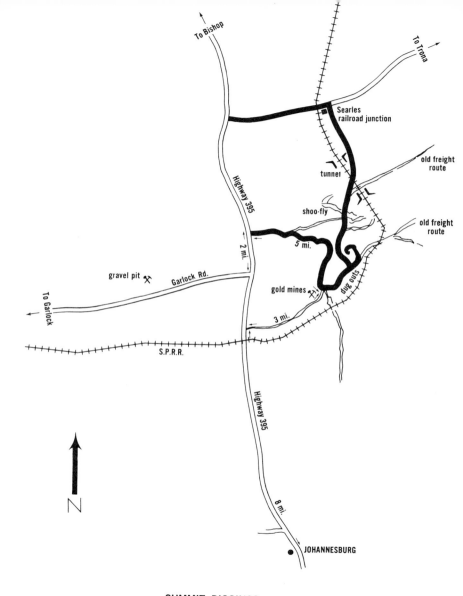

SUMMIT DIGGINGS

# 5. SUMMIT DIGGINGS

*A maze of roads, placer gold diggings, dugouts, and remains of an old railroad shoo-fly, best visited in cool weather, calls for experienced desert driving.*

Some adventurers climb mountains because they are there. Others enjoy following roads to see where they go. Summit Diggings is great for the road enthusiast as there are enough trails to provide exploring over a number of weekends and all within a few miles of a highway. Although this was primarily a gold area, not all roads were the result of mine operations. There is an old freight route for historians and artifact collectors plus camp sites and construction roads for the railroad buff.

Two roads go into the Summit. The easiest to locate is a dirt road to the right, east, off of Highway 395, just past a highway sign "Range Cattle," after topping the long hill eight miles north of Johannesburg. Keep to the well-used road tending toward the right; lesser used routes wander back into the main road but are usually rougher, sandy or both. They are for exploring after one becomes familiar with the lay of the land.

At one time the main road had so much use that the Automobile Club of Southern California posted their blue and white enamel signs at every cross road. They fell long ago under the hand of the marksman and vandal. For those who need reassurance those signs would still be helpful as only a few rods from the highway one gets the feeling of being miles away from everything. It is a satisfying bit of desert for those who like to get away from the crowd. If it is more comfortable to think of people being around then be assured that there are bike riders just over the

57

hill, campers tucked away behind a shielding bank, some hobby miners working their gold claims and from any high point, look west and traffic on Highway 395 is clearly visible.

Summit is a pie-shaped bit of desert bounded on two sides by hard surfaced highways and by the Southern Pacific railroad on the other. Three miles from the highway is the heart of gold country. In the early 1890's the area was crawling with prospectors and anyone that worked at all got some gold. Some were lucky and hit pockets of nuggets, some produced hardly enough to keep them in beans, bacon and tobacco while still others restlessly moved about hoping to find a better location and produced nothing at all.

The road takes broad curves and gradual inclines to wind through almost colorless and sparsely vegetated hills. Here and there an outcrop of green decomposed basalt catches the eye, a bright color in contrast to the rest of the hills. To the unpractised eye it would seem that a hill so green would have mineral wealth of some kind, but to the old time miners it was classed as "pure junkite."

Approximately five miles from the highway there is a distinct crossroad. A lone fireplace chimney, remains from a home that burned some years ago, is a good landmark and place to park for a look around. The fork to the right of the chimney goes through gold diggings that are still being worked. A short drive or walk to the diggings gives one a view of the immense amount of pick and shovel work that went into the process of securing gold. This was called "dry diggings" as there was no water and the material was put through a dry washer to shake away the dirt and gravel to leave nuggets and fine gold on the riffle board.

Follow this right angled road for three miles and you will be back to Highway 395 without seeing anything much except placer diggings, tailings and the rock outline of old tent home sites.

For real exploring skip the branch to the right and keep straight ahead toward the railroad tracks to a "Y." This branch to the right you can save for another trip. It goes under the tracks via a huge culvert and comes out into a small gold field where the clay matrix was like cement making the extraction of gold a difficult and expensive process. The road wanders through sage and greasewood to eventually come out on a hard surfaced road near Red Mountain. Years when rains are adequate wild-flowers carpet much of the washes and hillsides but other than that there is little of interest.

Take the left branch at the "Y" and follow the wash between the railroad tracks and a steep bank pitted with dugouts. A few years ago a mining company bulldozed back into this hillside and eliminated many of the dugouts which in the old days were a long row of openings that were living quarters for the miners and some families. They were in use as late as 1908-1912 when the railroad was built. One old timer recalled that as a small boy he traveled the "cushions" between Goler where his father was drilling a well and his mother at home near Brown. When the train reached the Summit dugouts it stopped if there was anyone getting on or off or there were grocery orders to unload. Heads would pop out of the dugouts to see who was arriving, or to wave at the engineer while children streaked across the wash and up the steep embankment to pick up the supplies being dropped. One of the engineers brightened the miner's day by 'quilling' as soon as he hit the area. The tunes he played on the old steam locomotive's whistle were not always identifiable but they were a beautiful sound floating out across the silent desert, and the days he made the run were special ones for the people of the Summit.

About a mile and a half from the "Y" a lone headframe looms up atop a small knob with a side wash splitting to go on each

*People lived in the dugouts that lined a cliff facing the railroad. Waving passengers and a delivery of groceries dropped off the passing train were highlights of the day.*

side. This was the first uranium discovery in the area that showed strong enough indications to warrant further exploration. That this is not uranium country is evident from limited amount of tailings.

There is a good level parking spot at the headframe and an ideal view of the mountains stretching off to the south and west. For the railroad buffs the short hike over to the tracks will reward them with a view of the steep grade that was a nightmare to the railroad construction engineers back in 1908. Here too is a place where "curve grease" is still in use.

Return to the wash below the headframe and continue on a short distance to another distinct crossroad, take the right hand road for a mile to dugouts on the west side of the hill. If someone hasn't already moved in, here is an ideal camping spot; a good road goes up to the level area in front of the dugout.

Shortly after World War I a veteran and his army nurse wife moved here where he had mine claims. In his spare time from mining and hauling water, the disabled veteran carved a home out of solid rock. Few early day desert homes were as cool in summer or warm in winter. A generator provided lights and power for a radio but it was still a lonely existence for the wife who was city raised. Sometimes the gold ran thin and the veteran's disability check was so small that they would be on the verge of starvation; other times the gold provided gas for the generator, food, kept the old car running and gave them a night of celebrating in the then wide open town of Red Mountain.

Leaving the dugout, backtrack to the crossroad and take the road to the right which travels to the west side of the hill where the veteran lived. Cross a "T" and continue on between two showy strawberry pink hills. Up a slight incline the road crosses an obvious old railroad bed which was part of a shoo-fly, or temporary tracks to get the train over El Paso Summit until a tunnel could be built. The tunnel was the longest in Southern Pacific history at that time, being 4,340 feet long. Built in 1909 it is still in use.

The shoo-fly made a roundabout trip along the mountain side and eventually got over the top. It took many engines as helpers and an unusual "Y" for them to reverse direction and return to the lower level ready to boost the next train over the top.

You can drive on the old shoo-fly a short distance on either side of the road, but areas are caving off. The best route is to go ahead approximately .03 of a mile, make a sharp turn to the right and you will be on the roadbed which goes through a cut and back to where you first crossed it. The sides are sloughing off in places and it may not be wide enough to travel for many more years, but it is no great distance to walk. Up on the level to the east of the old roadbed are signs of a construction camp or black-smith shop. A search would undoubtedly turn up collectables such as a four inch diameter washer with patent date May-10-04, found half embedded in the loose dirt. It takes days to follow all the old construction roads but along them are the temporary camp sites and discards of bottles, tins and metal scrap.

Above the shoo-fly is a "Y": the right branches off into an old freight road that edged around Searles Lake and headed for the Panamint mine camps. It stretches out across the desert with overnight camp sites about every ten miles. The ruts cut by the heavy wagons are a scar that has remained through the years and will for many more generations. The camp sites are usually recognizable by the sparse vegetation where the horses and mules grazed, rolled and stomped through the nights, and by the scattered broken glass, old liquor bottles, rusted condensed milk cans and the wide-mouthed sardine tins. Most of the old trail is not for passenger car travel.

If you take the left arm of the "Y" there will be a wood and barbed wire fence within a mile which indicates where the railroad tunnel surfaces. The right branch following down the fence travels toward the line of loaded freight cars. One may witness the Trona train pulling in with its load of chemicals or Southern Pacific engines busy switching cars in preparation of the haul out to Mojave. Chances are you will see the train going through the Summit or the tunnel but no one will quill you a tune for now the old steam locomotive, the prospectors and the creaking freight wagons are but a memory.

Down near the switching area is the hard surfaced road that goes north to Trona or left a short distance to dead end into Highway 395. A day or a weekend, the route has covered approximately twenty miles, leaving a multitude of beckoning roads for many more days of exploring.

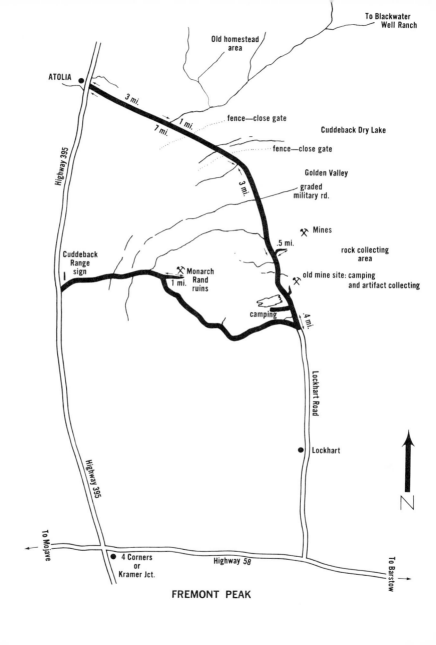

FREMONT PEAK

# 6. LOOP TRIP AROUND FREMONT PEAK

*From October to June this virtually undisturbed region is ideal for relaxing, getting acquainted with the land, the wild life, and oneself—plan a leisurely visit.*

---

Fremont Peak country has little that would be classed as spectacular scenery, but it does provide for a variety of interests and a wealth that lies in values for the restoration of man's well-being. Rare in today's world of southern California are two ingredients that abound in the peak area: space and quiet. There is little to interfere with the slight sound of displaced gravel, as a lizard darts for cover. Audible, too, is the soft swish of limber branches as greasewoods sway and bow to a passing breeze.

Overhead the desert raven and an occasional eagle circle and glide high and effortlessly on their own private air stream. Within reach, a Saw-Whet Owl humped on a Joshua limb pretends that no one is around, while sparrow, vireo, thrasher, or flycatcher cross and recross the trail in the daily business of acquiring food. It is a place of tranquility most of the time.

Fremont Peak itself rises steeply 4,584 feet above the floor of Golden Valley. The valley is believed to have received its name from the golden glow that appears at sunset. The peak, a landmark used by early travelers and the twenty mule team borax wagon men, was named for John C. Fremont during the 1850's when his popularity was running high. His name marked not only outstanding peaks but graced canyons, counties, and towns in over a hundred different places. One by one the name was changed to that of a local hero or a more favored identification;

*Pulverized ore spilling down the hill, sun and wind scarred wood are part of the Rand-Monarch mine on the side of Fremont Peak.*

by 1900 Fremont Peak and a railroad siding opposite it along the Randsburg Railroad were the only legally recognized places still carrying the Fremont name in all of California. Gradually the name is reappearing along the route of his early travels.

Today the peak that can be seen for miles stands rugged and rocky sided, inviting and challenging those who like to climb mountains, explore in search of little known plant life, untouched rock and mineral deposits or the haunts of small wild life.

Twenty-five miles north of the junction of State 58 and U.S. Highway 395, at Four Corners (or Kramer Junction), is the little mining settlement of Atolia. A dirt road used by any type of vehicle leaves the highway near the north end of the cluster of buildings and heads northeast between a few ancient houses. The route curves between tungsten mines, dumps and abandoned headframes, some of which date back to World War I. This is private property and one should not leave the road without permission of the mining company at Atolia. Actually there is little need to leave the road; the colorful tailing piles, aged wood frames and mine pits are as interesting and photographically challenging, viewed from the traveled path as they would be from any other point.

Keep in an easterly direction on the well-used road, taking the right branch at each "Y" for three miles. Just past a concrete tank on the right the route swings south, heading straight for Fremont Peak. The left roads are not for passenger cars as they branch out to old homestead plots, mining projects and eventually end up at Blackwater Ranch or against the Navy reservation, at the side of the ranch. Most of the area is private property, patrolled by cowboys who not only herd cattle but keep pumps running at a number of watering places. For the off-the-road vehicle the dim trails follow old line fences, and end up at former homestead sites, recognized by rusted metal, twisted fencing,

67

metal sheeting, so shot up that it gives the appearance of having gone through a great battle, and sand blasted old post leaning away from the wind.

The route to Fremont Peak travels a section of the cattle country, too, and in spring the carpet of green gives credence to its use as range land but in winter there is a bareness that belies this use. Teepee shaped bunches of dry, coarse grass are hardly noticeable to the inexperienced eye, yet they dot the valley and are rich in nutrition as cattle feed. If the fence gates are up, close them behind you.

Stay on the well used road heading for the peak, ignoring crossroads that are graded for use by army, air force or high line maintenance. Creosote bushes grow close to the road and, like a welcoming committee, will reach in an open car window or slide along an unsuspecting arm resting on the window ledge. This is an old route used by wagons many yesterdays ago; there was no need for a wide path then as there is no need for one today.

Nearing the foot of Fremont Peak, follow the contour of the mountain on the southeast side, or to the left at about twelve miles from the departure point at Atolia. The well worn trail goes between the peak, on the right, and colorful volcanic hills, on the left. A short half mile side trip into these hills branches left opposite a startlingly smooth, cream colored playa at the base of Fremont Peak. The road into the hills grows narrow and faint past the half mile point; passenger cars should turn around here, four-wheel-drive vehicles can continue on to an abandoned mineral prospect.

The turn around point offers a sheltered spot to camp and unique geological contrasts to explore. On one side is pastel colored, chalk-like material. The yellow is Sinter deposited out of an ancient steam vent, the gray is diorite, a blend of granite and banded rhyolite. The opposite side of the road is steep, rough and a composition of dark volcanic rock where flesh colored feldspar is just starting to erode out to the surface. There is a definite indication of a pegmetite dyke, quartz crystals forming and some hornblende crystals. A search should turn up garnet. There are more hills to explore and a bit of digging could uncover a virgin field for crystal and mineral collectors.

Here is an ideal place for beginning geologists or student field trips, for within this small area is visual evidence of recent volcanic action, steam vent deposits, cinder cone rhyolite, older igneous intrusions and every form of quartz. A fine example of an alluvial fan comes down from Fremont Peak to a playa of clay that is hard and smooth when dry, soft and sticky when wet.

Other roads branch off into the pink and tan hills for those who wish to explore the geological wonders. Within a mile of the first described side trip, keep to the right at a distinct "Y," which in turn will curve to the left around a large playa or dry lake. Old placer diggings and remains of a mill border the lake. For the relic collector there are interesting shapes in rusted iron, for the antique car enthusiast there are rusted fenders and car parts dating back to the 20's and somewhere within walking distance should be the cook house dump for a bottle collectors' dig. Photographers will find the ruins, the prospect holes, and the crackled pattern of the dried silt, demanding subject matter.

When there have been winter rains the narrow cuts, between the hills and the valley, between Fremont Peak and the volcanic area, become wild flower gardens with a wide variety of plants. Though desert climatic conditions are severe, plant life has developed devices for continued existence and some bloom each year regardless of the lack of moisture. Most have protective coats on their seeds so that there will be no germination until conditions are just right, regardless of the years of waiting. Variation in the spring display is not only influenced by moisture, the elevation

69

*Old structures that played an important part in the process of mining stand silent, sun dried and wind carved, monuments to a past of wealth.*

and soil also play a part. What will grow at one elevation does not appear at other heights and practically none will survive out of their natural habitat. For the naturalist this area has much of interest. There are still unidentified plants to be discovered and hundreds of mini-flowers that have drawn little or no attention though they are extremely beautiful, when viewed through a magnifying glass.

The road skirts the left side of the dry playa, but at points may be difficult to see due to a confusion of motorcycle tracks. It is easily picked up again on the south side and continues in a south-easterly direction. Within a mile of the old mine site, a side road to the right goes into a sheltered cove that is a delightful camping spot. Camping on the east side of Fremont Peak, the sheltered side since the prevailing winds are out of the northwest, is a do-it-yourself proposition with only level spots developed by nature. Food, water, fuel and shelter must be carried in and refuse carried out.

From this particular cove there is a view of a long valley reaching to the horizon and the distant settlements of Lockhart and Hinkley, where the old road terminated for travelers coming this way before the turn of the century. No doubt they too found this a pleasant place to camp and enjoyed the same kind of wonderful nights that bring the stars almost within touching distance, so large and bright in the immense sky. With no highrises to shut out or distort, the wonder of the earth's movement can be witnessed as the full moon appears at the edge of the horizon. The moon, like the stars, seems so large with its light so bright.

If there is no conversation or human movement the little night people with bright eyes, sensitive whiskers and long tails will start to move about. In time they will move in close, tempted by the smell of crumbs or water and their antics will provide hours of unusual entertainment.

A mile from the camp site the main road branches; keep to the left for four tenths of a mile and then take the right hand road which is better than the one a short way back that turned in the same direction. The left branch is the Lockhart road and in approximately eighteen miles reaches State Highway 58.

The route to the right continues along the foothills of Fremont Peak. Side roads branch off to prospect holes; one is marked by the rusted carcass of an old bus which can be seen from the main road. The entrance to the prospect, just back of the bus, is an example of a discovery that was good enough to encourage the prospector to do considerable digging in hopes of picking up a rich deposit. When nothing good turned up, the project was abandoned. But not without the gamble that the next foot of excavation could prove a bonanza or just a more tired back and blistered hands.

The next five miles follow the contour of the mountain. Vegetation changes as does the terrain. Reefs of slate, like the humps and spines of some prehistoric animal, curve along the high ridges, entirely different than the opposite side of the peak.

A well-used road to the right goes a mile to the ruins of the old Monarch Rand mine, once an active camp built around a rich gold and tungsten strike. The remains indicate how extensive the operation had been with a mill, settling tanks and ore chutes. Operated in the early 1900's and again in the 1960's, it is an interesting place to camp and explore. Texture of weathered wood, wind eroded tailings, and tired, leaning structures are for artist and photographers. Small unsorted ore piles hold specimen material for rock collectors and somewhere in a nearby gully there should be a treasure of old bottles, but it will take some looking since the discards from the recent operation will have covered the older artifacts. This is hardly a place to expect rewards in a quick look around and since Monarch Rand is on the wind-

72

ward side of Fremont Peak it can be so uncomfortably cold that any treasure hunting is out of the question at the moment.

From Monarch Rand the trail heads west and is frequently intersected by good graded roads most of which are for military use but will take you on around the mountain to the east side and the route you have just traveled. It is seven miles straight out to Highway 395 and the sign that reads "Cuddleback Range." Approximately ten miles to the right is Atolia, the starting point; the nearest gas and water is three miles farther north. To the left on Highway 395, in about the same distance, is Four Corners, with supplies, accommodations, and traffic. The quiet, relaxed mood country will be but a memory.

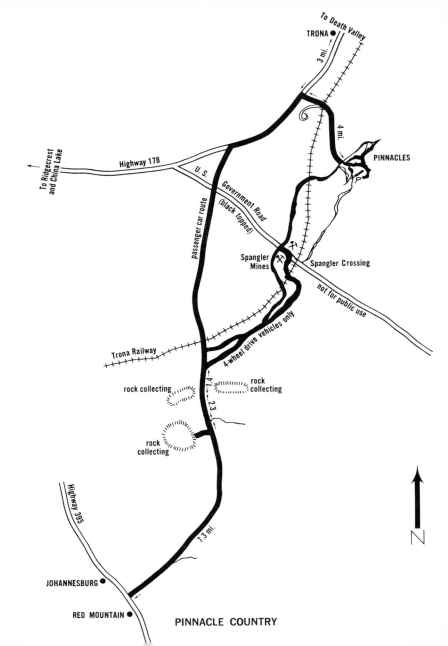

To Death Valley

TRONA ●

3 mi.

4 mi.

PINNACLES

Highway 178

To Ridgecrest and China Lake

U.S. Government Road (black topped)

passenger car route

Spangler Mines

Spangler Crossing

not for public use

Trona Railway

4-wheel drive vehicles only

rock collecting

1.4

rock collecting

2.3

rock collecting

Highway 395

7.3 mi.

JOHANNESBURG ●

RED MOUNTAIN ●

PINNACLE COUNTRY

N

# 7. PINNACLE COUNTRY

*Take off from reality and experience a hidden world of weird shapes and moving shadows. A one-way in and out passenger car trip or loop through the desert for more rugged vehicles to be enjoyed during dry, cool weather.*

Some years ago, before our astronauts had conquered space, 20th Century Fox used the Pinnacle country for a science fiction movie with scenes of the first family landing on the moon. Movie patrons thought the whole thing was out of this world; in reality anyone with a taste for adventure can enjoy this moon-like land without the discomfort of a space suit.

Fascinating figures, domes and steeples of white, tans, browns, faded red and gray cover an area over ten miles long and four miles wide. Depending on the time of day and lighting, the unique formations present an ever changing panorama enhanced by shadow patterns. Visitors see many likenesses in the assortment of shapes and have named the larger ones: The Monk, Owl, Eagle and Dog, but the resemblances show only at certain times of the day, otherwise they appear as objects unknown to earth people.

An interesting area to explore many times, the Pinnacles lie between Red Mountain and Trona, dividing the stark white of Searles Lake from the tan-to-rose tones of the Mojave Desert. There is a well-defined road from the highway that is used by passenger cars but the longer, back country route has a great deal more to offer in scenery, and historic ruins.

Leave Highway 395, one mile north of Red Mountain, at the sign indicating the turn off to Trona and Death Valley. A good, hard surfaced road stretches out toward the valley and the blue haze of distant mountains. Near the summit, at seven and three tenths miles from the junction, a dirt road drops off to the left.

*Moving shadows and changing light give the Pinnacles an air of fantasy.*

This side trail is hard packed, fine for car, camper, or small trailer and leads into a miniature canyon of volcanic pinks, tans and rich brick red. The area is an old gem rock picking field that has been searched for years yet still produces good, colorful cutting material. For the collector or non-collector the canyon is a delightful camping spot, fairly secluded yet within a few feet of the road.

The terrain is sloping and the low rolling hills are for easy walking with an ever changing material underfoot. For the rock collector there are small pieces, two to three cab size, variegated red agate with dendrite, good white banded yellow jasper with brown, red or green plume. Jasp-agate from transparent to red, tan, deep wine with traces of green and yellow continuously erode out near an outcrop of Basalt containing very small agate geodes to the west of the road. Interesting green and red jasper is exposed in the low gray hills to the left near the entrance to the area; looks promising for one with an inclination to dig below the weathered top.

The amount of material to be found depends on the rate of erosion and this is not the place to collect large chunks or any great amount, but who needs a ton anyway; it takes too many life times to work up!

Two and three tenths miles farther along the main highway a ridge of decomposed jasper and agate can be seen on either side of the road. To the casual observer this is an uninteresting appearing jumble of broken rock, but for the collector with a fluorescent light there is the beauty of bright green, orange, and red that is hidden from the naked eye.

One and a half miles from this point or eleven miles from the junction of Highway 395, a dirt road turns right, before the main route crosses the railroad tracks. This is where modern cars with their soft springs will continue on the main highway while off-the-road vehicles take to the dirt trail. The dirt road is traveled by passenger cars but should not be attempted unless the driver is

*At one time of day this formation in the Pinnacles resembles a
poodle, but in a few minutes the change of lighting makes it into
an ape and from another point of view it resembles a pug-nosed
human.*

familiar with desert driving and his vehicle capable of maneuvering a few sharp dips. Though there are neither high centers nor deep sand, the once sharply defined road is now paralleled, crisscrossed, cut up and almost obliterated in spots by cycle tracks, making it difficult to remain on the right path. The main route angles northeast for six miles along the south side of the railroad tracks.

The rails that the road parallels is the Trona Railroad, one of the few short lines left in operation in the United States. It was built when mule team freighting could no longer haul borax in competition with companies near railroads. The Southern Pacific line was thirty-two miles away (see Summit trip) and neither they nor any other company wanted to risk investing in a road to Trona where borax was being mined. The Trona company was desperate, as their whole future hinged on transporting their product to the main line at a reasonable cost.

In spite of harassment by claim jumpers, legal battles over claim boundaries, labor problems created by the many races working at the lake and the need for plant development, the struggling young company decided to build their own line. Unlike most railroad construction of that time, there was no ribbon cutting, band playing, toast drinking, colorful ground breaking ceremony. Different, too, was the fact that on September 27th, 1913, the wife of the company president, Mrs. Joseph Hutchinson did the ground breaking. Dressed in high fashion, with large decorative hat, long sleeved blouse and a skirt that swept the ground she trudged behind a plow in the shimmering desert heat. The team of mules raised a cloud of dust that covered her beautiful attire and sand seeped in her high button shoes. Though the ceremony was unorthodox, the railroad thrived, outlived many of the big lines and today hauls chemical wealth over its well kept thirty-two miles of track.

Driving within sight of the rails most of the time, the visitor can mentally picture the early day train with its immense steam engines, open windowed coaches, men standing in the open door of the mail car and others walking across the top of freight cars. The picturesque steam locomotive with its mixed load was replaced by diesel power in 1948, but if one is fortunate enough to be in the area when the short line train goes through it will seem that old Number 2 is still in use. A white cloud flows back of the locomotive and along the ridge of cars like billowing smoke from a steam locomotive. The impression is the result of powdered chemicals whirling into the air from some of the open gondolas.

Thousands of tons of Soda Ash, Chlorides of Soda, Lithium, Pyro Borate, Borax and many by-products are hauled on this route daily. The old time table and schedule listed stops for ore shipments and passengers at Trona, Borosolvay (now West End), Rock Crusher, Hanksite, Pinnacle, Spangler and Searles. The only stops today between West End and Searles are in the spring when grazing sheep move out of the wind into sheltered coves and onto the tracks, or at night when a herd of wild burro decides to feed on the other side of the tracks, stringing out in plodding determination that brings the heavy loaded cars to a stand still.

If you have stayed on the old route you will cross the railroad tracks at a railroad sign "Spangler." In this area you will find the Spangler ruins where two brothers, Rea and Tony, spent the major portions of their lives digging by hand thousands of feet in underground tunnels. The gold they brought out was never enough to make them wealthy, but paid for food and supplies, and was sufficient to tease them into making "just one more try." By following the newer route you will miss the ruins and cross the tracks a mile sooner, putting you on the north side.

From this point north, lumps of rough, porous looking rock begin to appear. In the distance can be seen larger formations marching along the rim of a smooth basin. Freighters skirted those

80

formations a hundred years ago. Seeing a resemblance to church steeples, they called the place Cathedral City. Later the official name, Pinnacles, appeared on maps.

These unique formations were built up under a lake when the area was tropical and fresh water flowed into the sink now known as Searles Dry Lake. The ancient beach line is visible about seven hundred feet above the present desert and dry lake surface. Scientists do not agree entirely on the development of these porous spurs, but in general they describe the Pinnacles as having been built under water by blue-green algae, minute organisms growing one upon another, forming the shapes that stand dry and rough surfaced along the desert floor.

For the passenger car traveler, the trip to the same area is thirty-three miles from the highway junction out of Red Mountain. A right turn onto a dirt road at the highway sign "End 178" passes a large yellow sign that in Spanish and English warns of no gas or maintenance ahead. The road is well traveled as Trona residents are frequent visitors to the Pinnacles. Within a little over a mile the road crosses the Trona railroad tracks and a sharp right hand turn (there is usually a "Pinnacle" sign at this point) takes the visitor to the picturesque formations in less than four miles. The route crosses a lake bed that is slippery when wet making it advisable to visit during dry weather, and since it follows the rolling contour of the land, speed exceeding twenty miles per hour is not practical in many places.

A maze of roads weave in and out of the formations giving ever changing viewpoints. Morning and evening coloring is the most intense and the long blue shadows of the late or early hours adds much to the beauty of the area. This is moon country without a space suit or the trauma of a splash down, with the highway only five miles away and a choice of left to Red Mountain and Ridgecrest or right to Trona with its modern facilities and supplies for an extended trip to Death Valley.

81

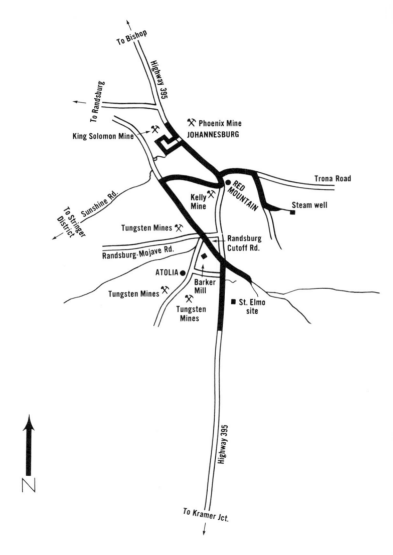

To Bishop

Highway 395

To Randsburg

✕ Phoenix Mine
JOHANNESBURG

King Solomon Mine ↗ ⚒

Sunshine Rd.

To Stringer District

Kelly Mine ⚒

● RED MOUNTAIN

Trona Road

■ Steam well

Tungsten Mines ⚒

Randsburg-Mojave Rd.

Randsburg Cutoff Rd.

ATOLIA ●

Barker Mill

Tungsten Mines ⚒

Tungsten Mines ⚒

■ St. Elmo site

Highway 395

To Kramer Jct.

N

**ATOLIA, RED MOUNTAIN AND JOHANNESBURG**

# 8. ATOLIA, RED MOUNTAIN, AND JOHANNESBURG

*In and around desert towns that are but a faint shadow of their flourishing beginnings.*

Remember the last time you slowed down to a posted speed limit and loafed through the few blocks of a small town, all the while wondering why it existed?

There are a number of such miniature communities along Highway 395 as it climbs northward to skirt the east side of the Sierras. Outwardly most of them show little to entice the traveler into taking time out from his rush to some distant destination, yet each has its story, points of interest and reason for being. Usually the settlements are many miles apart or at least a day's travel by team and wagon; an exception is a cluster of four desert communities separated by only two to four miles.

From junction of the east-west artery State 58 and U.S. Highway 395 at Kramer (Four Corners) the route north cuts through miles of seemingly uninhabited desert. Fremont Peak on the right, Red Mountain almost straight ahead and the Boron Air Force facilities on the left are all that break up the sameness of near-level desert acres. The modern, high speed road parallels the old road bed of a Santa Fe railroad branch that took one hour and twenty-five minutes for the run of twenty-eight-and-a-half miles into the gold, silver and tungsten country. The first stop for water, freight and passengers was Fremont, almost opposite the mountain by the same name.

Eight miles farther was St. Elmo that is marked now by the rusted remains of tin cans, and bits of broken glass two miles south of Atolia. Fifty years ago that area became the largest tungsten producing field in the world and St. Elmo faded out as Atolia became the center of activity. One of the four closely related settlements, Atolia has boomed and died more than once depending on the need for tungsten and through it all miners kept some of the buildings in repair, hung onto their leases and hoped for prices that compensated for their labor.

A few years ago a large mining concern reactivated the mines, the mill and miners' skills. Air hoses again hiss with the force of air being pushed into the mines, water goes in and out of the shafts and electricity on each level of working tunnels improves greatly on the dim glow of the miners carbide light combating the dense underground darkness. Trucks rumble upgrades bringing in ore; there is the whine of hoists, the crunch of rock being pulverized and the sounds of voices mingle in a setting of old building nearing collapse and new metal structures housing present day technology.

The handful of buildings that is Atolia, lies on both sides of the highway. A gate on the right closes off the operations section and a cable on the left shuts an old road leaving only an entrance to the company offices. On the right just a short distance from the metal gate is a dirt road that dips off the highway and heads for more mining country, an operating cattle spread, abandoned homestead sites, Fremont Peak, and military reservations; all of which are another area to explore (see Chapter 6).

For a short mile trip into the immediate area, follow the well-used path, especially if there have been rains which tend to cut a small wash; local residents with cars and pickup trucks use this route daily. In less than a mile the road curves along the edge of a pit and buildings which are the Old Spanish Mine seen in National Geographic's Mojave Desert T.V. special of a few years ago. Just beyond the mine is a picturesque head frame on the

84

opposite side of the road with adequate space for parking and turning. Here in the rows of cone shaped mounds and man-made canyons, wealth in tungsten was produced.

The Old Spanish Mine, one of the first big strikes in the field, was discovered and developed by a group of Spanish speaking miners who kept to themselves, took out a fortune and departed. Various miners worked the existing tunnels and added more; some did well, others found little for their trouble and some died of injuries from falling rock. Search for a new ore bed was in full swing at the time of the National Geographic filming and signs of a possible bonanza were present but further blasting failed to locate that which was not seen but hoped for, and the miners moved on in the continuous quest for a pay streak. Tomorrow it will be leased to someone else who has a theory as to where the values lie and that may be the one to hit the jackpot, and set off another mining boom. Maybe he will quit a winner but more than likely history will repeat itself with the earnings poured back into the ground in the hope that a still richer deposit will be found.

Back on Highway 395, a few feet beyond the dirt road, is part of a foundation that marks the site of the one time Donker's Sunshine Dairy known for its non-fat milk long before that type of milk was an accepted product. Though mothers worried about the value to their children there was little they could do except complain as fresh milk was a scarce item on the desert. Interesting jugs with sturdy bales and an occasional glass milk bottle with name intact can be found whole, having been protected by the over hanging branches of native bushes.

Within the next mile the old Santa Fe road bed is plainly visible on the right as is the scattered dump of the early 1900's that in recent years became a favored hunting ground for relic hunters.

Upon the hill to the left is the Barker Mill, built many years ago by one of the Barker brothers of the well known Los Angeles

*Remains of the Kelly Silver mine buildings and tailings as seen from Highway 395. Silver ore was so rich here that men rode shotgun on the wagons that hauled it the few feet from the mine to the mill. South edge of Red Mountain.*

merchants. Like the Atolia mining, the mill has been in operation off and on, depending on the market for tungsten. Almost in line with the mill is a dirt road that climbs to the mill, and continues a few feet farther to a better, graded road at the square white sign post indicating Randsburg Cut Off in black lettering. The cut off gives a good view of the mill on the left and to the right the spectacular structures associated with the Kelly Silver Mine and mill on the outskirts of Red Mountain.

In a mile a left branch near a cluster of buildings curves back of Atolia and ends at the cable closed entrance to the highway. From this old oil-surfaced Atolia road there are numerous good, car-passable, dirt roads that wander through miles of diggings, dumps and pass an occasional camp site where a diligent search usually turns up an aged sun-purpled bottle, a tobacco tin, discarded toy or heavy miner's pick minus the wooden handle.

Instead of going toward Atolia one can take the branch to the right which is Butte, continuation of Randsburg's main street of the same name. There are abandoned buildings, mines, prospects and scattered habitation for the next mile. At the oiled road make a sharp right and follow it to the Kelly Mine and Highway 395 at Red Mountain. The Kelly was a large, rich silver operation that supported its own mill. Well-built company houses are still occupied and kept in good repair by local residents. The buildings of the milling operation stand in ruins, gaunt silhouettes against the clear desert sky. Their apparent abandonment, however, belies the recent testing and plans to go into operation with modern methods when the price of silver rises to a point that will make mining again possible.

The skeleton of the large building, the cream colored sump, and the molded residue left by dismantled tanks, offer the photographer, amateur or professional, an immense variety to record on film.

87

*A frames, loading chutes, mine dumps, abandoned mill buildings and rusted metal encroach upon the tiny community of Red Mountain.*

The Kelly developed from a fabulously rich silver deposit that gold seekers had been stumbling over for years while trying to eke out a living. Some of the men were nearly starving on the little gold they could produce while at the same time they were throwing away and cussing the dark, troublesome metal that interfered with their work. It was in 1919 that two able prospectors had samples assayed that were so high in silver content that it left California gasping and set off another boom in an area already famous for its gold and tungsten. Typical of mining discoveries, the miners poured in hoping to find a small bit of unclaimed land to work for themselves or get in on the jobs opening with the growing company. Most settled for jobs and happy to be at work in the business they knew best; mining was slow all over the west and miners had found it difficult to stay employed.

The Kelly welcomed the miners, and though there were no living accomodations, that condition changed with unbelievable speed. Tents were pitched in scattered disarray, empty buildings from Johannesburg, Randsburg and as far away as Garlock were cut into movable pieces and rushed to the scene. Even before they were off the moving-timbers buildings went into use and a line of business places formed along an unplanned street.

The boom brought in all types of men; highgrading of the rich silver was an accepted fact, fights were the order of the day and shootings frequently went unnoticed. Water was scarce but a drink of liquor could be obtained every place except the post office, where there were problems enough without serving drinks.

As the population burgeoned a feud developed between two factions. Pete Osdick, a long time resident miner who had been scratching for gold almost on the door step of the Kelly, attempted to build an orderly, law abiding settlement named Osdick. The other faction tended toward the wild roaring mine camp pattern and went by various names including Inn City and Sin City.

*A field of desert candles grows along the road to the steam wells.*
*A squaw cabbage, the lower leaves are edible, tasting like spinach.*
*The hollow yellow green stem supports, small, purple, pea-shaped*
*blooms.*

The post office, caught in the middle of the controversy and trying to settle on one name for mail delivery, finally disregarded local feeling and using the imposing mountain overlooking all the activity, called it Red Mountain. If the outside world or new comers gave it any thought the name probably seemed appropriate but some of the local residents resented the postal high-handedness to their dying day.

By whatever name one wanted to call it, the town was a wild, wide open place resembling the old mine camps of the late 1800's. Liquor flowed freely until word came that the "revonoers" were coming to make a raid; the shut down lasted only until the law was seen going down the dusty road. Madams ran houses that were small replicas of the Barbary Coast days and clients came from as far away as Los Angeles. The dance hall girls were pretty and as one bar tender recalled, "They were mostly brunettes, a few red heads and no blonds."

Time and fires have wiped out much of Red Mountain's wild past; the mine buildings, the dumps of green, gold, blue and pink and a few miners' shacks that have been modernized are of that past. Saloons, hotels and cribs that were the town's backbone of activity are mostly gone or changed beyond recognition, of which the Owl Saloon and Hotel is one and the Silver Dollar, a replacement that saw only the dwindling action at the end of the boom era, is another.

Just out of Red Mountain one can take a short side trip to a steam vent that sits in colorful hills built by thermal action. North of town a road to the right leaves Highway 395 for Trona and Death Valley. A mile from the main highway turn right on a dirt trail that can be traversed by auto but has rough spots that demand low gear driving. Four miles on this road and then a left turn to the pastel toned hills and a small building. A number of years ago the steam was channeled into a pipe and the local citizenry had their own private steam baths. From a tent to an abandoned school bus the bath house was whatever was handy to contain the steam which was increased by the addition of water poured down the open mouthed pipe. A recent ambitious project that included a roofed building, individual rooms and storage tank was so vandalized that the work was discontinued. There is still steam, and with a bit of imagination an improvised bath house can provide the visitor with a unique desert experience. The road beyond the steam well is not for passenger cars but a pickup or four-wheel drive can go on through to Cuddeback Dry Lake country, through an old ranch that is reputed to have been a lively place during prohibition.

A mile north of the Trona junction, Highway 395 enters Johannesburg, the only settlement of the four closely related mining communities that was planned rather than let grow, hit or miss. In the early years its greatest boast was the golf club where members played a course that ran around the outskirts of the town. It must have been an interesting sight as men in caps and knickers, women in long skirts, high necked blouses and wide brimmed hats battled the wind and sand to the tune of the heavy thumping beat of gold mills hammering rock into dust.

A left turn at the old St. Charles Hotel takes one past Teagle's store from which supplies were freighted to the mine camps in the Panamints, Skidoo and Death Valley. Appearing to be part of the same building but with a different false front, is what had been Harrison's Saloon where shooting scrapes were always in self defense and Harrison was justified in doing whatever he wished.

At the intersection of Panamint Street is a house that originally was the top half of the railroad station and surprisingly it has lost none of its depot look. Higher up the hill, Fremont Street, to the right, swings around the cemetery that for seventy-five years has served the desert for miles around. Sand blasted wooden head boards and ornate iron fences stand in contrast to the more recent ornate rock work erected in memory of Shady Myrick, the discoverer of Myrickite, a gem rock much desired by rock collectors. Another pretentious edifice nearby is for Burro Schmidt, the man who spent a good portion of his lifetime digging a tunnel through a mountain in the El Paso Range.

Beyond the cemetery is the remains of the once great King Solomon mine that was discovered in 1896. Exact gold output is unknown but record shows that between 1919 and 1942 it produced approximately $500,000 with gold running $25 per ton of ore from its vast underground network that reaches to the Big Butte Mine in Randsburg. Silence engulfs the place today and one's foot step will echo through the empty buildings where noise, crushed rock, dust, shouting men and the grind of machinery live only in memory.

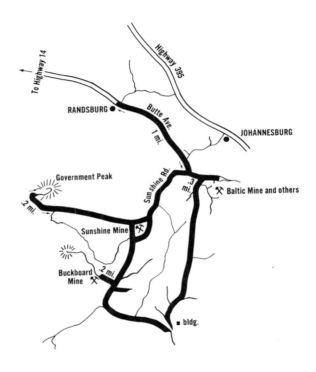

To Highway 14

Highway 395

RANDSBURG

Butte Ave.

1 mi.

JOHANNESBURG

Government Peak

Sun shine Rd.

.3 mi.

Baltic Mine and others

.2 mi.

Sunshine Mine

Buckboard Mine

.2 mi.

bldg.

N

**STRINGER DISTRICT**

# 9. STRINGER DISTRICT AND GOVERNMENT PEAK

*This area, like a majority of the Mojave Desert, is best explored during cool weather. Passenger cars can safely travel most of the roads; directions are indicated where trails are for more sturdy vehicles.*

---

An almost unbelievably short time ago, less than eighty five years, few men had put foot on the Rand Mountains. There were no wagon wheel ruts or mine scars, not even a name. Wild plants and animal life thrived undisturbed in the valley, along the ridges and down the multi-forked washes.

The whole scene changed in 1895 with the discovery of gold on the north side of the unexplored range. What was to become the famous Yellow Aster Mine triggered an influx of prospectors that spread through the canyon and swarmed over the hills sampling rock, running gravel through dry washers or with just a shovel and gold pan, decided where they thought a fortune may lay hidden.

A high, cone-shaped pile of rock marked each corner of the chunk of desert each man or group of men selected. Mine claims like the squares, triangles and oblong pieces of a patchwork quilt covered miles of mountains, canyons and washes. Some found enough gold to warrant extensive development but the majority of the men flowing into the area had to settle for jobs in established mines or move on to continue their restless search for the illusive metal.

A trip from the main street of Randsburg to the opposite side of the mountain is to travel the ghost country of gold dominated years. The Stringer District is a visual example of man's determination to wrest wealth from the earth. The pitted and bruised land is mute evidence of gold's relentless power.

As Butte Avenue climbs to the outskirts of town it passes between a couple of one-time sizeable mine operations. Big Butte stretches along the mountain side on the left and Consolidated pushes up a draw on the right. Travel east through the now silent Fiddler's Gulch. The few standing head frames, eroded tailings and tunnel openings are small reminders of the boom days when men, teams, dynamite blasts and the continuous thump of stamp mills made it a busy, noisy place.

One mile from Randsburg, swing to the right on the oil surfaced Sunshine Road and within a mile leave the hard top for another right onto a good maintained dirt road. On top of the hill to the left are the remains of the Sunshine Mine. An old tank, tailing piles and vandalized shaft are all that is left of an operation that followed a six to twelve inch wide, six hundred foot deep vein of gold-bearing quartz.

Wheat sized grains of gold, some of the largest mined in the Rand Mountains were brought out of the Sunshine from 1896 to 1915. A three stamp mill and cyanide plant processed the ore that ran one and a half ounces of gold per ton of ore and produced $1,000,000 in the nineteen year period.

The well-used road to the right of the Sunshine makes a gradual climb for little over a mile to a level parking area that lies less than a half mile from the crest of Government Peak. This 4,755 foot high point in the Rand Range bristles with towers that are a part of governmental and telephone communications system. Though the road continues to the peak and the fenced structures, there is little space for parking or turning around so it is advisable to walk up if one desires a view from the top, which has little advantage over the panorama seen from the lower level.

In either case the scene is like an aerial photo that encompasses great distances and offers a new perspective of the country to be explored.

To the far northwest is the snow-topped southern portion of the Sierras; closer in the El Paso Mountains running northeast to southwest, skirting the flat expanse of Fremont Valley. Miles of desert tan are interrupted by the white of Koehn Dry Lake, small green squares of alfalfa, dark clumps of tamarisk trees and the thin lines that mark old freight routes or the more recent trails cut by off-the-road vehicles.

On either side of Government Peak can be seen abandoned mine camps that cling to the mountain side and can be reached only by narrow foot or wagon trails. The buildings are collapsing, tunnels caving and erosion is eating away the long unused roads. Any one of them would be an interesting place to visit if one is inclined to enjoy long distance hiking over rough, steep terrain punctuated by slide areas.

To the east a lone peak rising out of a gold-toned expanse of Cuddeback Dry Lake and Golden Valley is the early explorer's landmark, Fremont Peak. Blue haze and indistinct mountains, seventy miles away, are the San Bernardino Mountains forming a border along the edge of this desert picture.

From Government Peak there is a choice of routes but for the most interesting mine workings and passenger car travel it is advisable to return to within a few feet of the oil topped Sunshine Road and turn right on a worn dirt trail. If the right hand dirt route is missed then three tenths of a mile farther on another right hand road takes off of the Sunshine Road. Within a half mile there is considerable evidence of mining on all sides.

This is a good place to park and explore on foot. In accordance with the law all abandoned mine excavations have been covered, closed and fenced but there are thoughtless individuals who remove covers, make campfires out of the fencing and tear down tunnel closures. The danger is minimal but it takes only one fall to spoil a trip. Counsel children against running or straying away from adults. Common sense dictates the futility of standing on the edge of a hole to peer down into black nothingness.

The area so extensively mined, was composed of a network of narrow veins or stringers carrying gold and tungsten throughout an otherwise non-metallic rock mass. The veins, though usually rich in ore, were not only narrow but were frequently offset or broken by fault lines. Considerably extra digging had to be done in search of stringers that suddenly stopped. It took all of a miner's past experience, some guess work and a good portion of luck, hope and hard work in sleuthing underground for that lost thread of ore.

Right in the center of a cluster of abandoned mine campsites reposes a "Rube Goldberg" dry washer of recent vintage. A few years ago an enterprising individual tried working here when it seemed the price of tungsten would make it a profitable venture. Either the price wasn't right, the ore not good enough or the work too demanding so the project was abandoned. The dry washer is a unique combination of past and present that would jolt a mechanically mined individual into laughter or tears.

Heavily worked from 1896 to 1918, the area is not only strewn with old wood and rusted metal, but broken pieces of sun purpled glass suggests that old bottles and other artifacts may be buried in the gullies or within throwing distance of old cabin sites. At present there is little evidence of relic digging, yet occupancy dates back to the liquor, cod liver oil and patent medicine period that quickens the pulse of the bottle collector.

Almost as interesting as the ruins, are some of the mine names that run the full gamut from the unimaginative G. B. Mine, to the more colorful Orphan Girl, Winnie, Red Bird, Sophie Moren,

Pearl Wedge, Ben Hur and Tam-O-Shanter. The Gold Crown, Gold Coin, Gold King, Victory Wedge, and Golden Eagle seemed to be more wishful than actual.

From this mine-pitted locality the road continues south-westerly through scattered workings and rock cabin ruins. It is a firm surfaced trail but a couple of short dips within the next mile are sharp enough to cause low slung passenger car rear bumpers to scrape. For those continuing beyond this point there is directional assurance in the almost continuous view on the right, of the Los Angeles Water and Power Company transmitter on top of Rand Peak. Lesser used roads branch to the right into more abandoned diggings and an area that carries highgrade manganese with rhodonite, most of which is on privately owned claims.

At the point where another well-defined road crosses take the right branch for one fourth mile to the picturesque Buckboard Mine tucked back in the opening to a narrow canyon. A complete headframe silhouettes against the distant valley on one side and sage covered banks on the other. Three openings to incline shafts smile defiance at explorer, photographer and relic collector. The shafts slant to a four hundred fifty foot depth plus two thousand feet of drifts all of which add up to a lot of underground blasting and digging. The miners followed a gold bearing fault along a footwall of a rhyolite dike that produced $500,000 in gold and an unknown amount of tungsten.

From the old Buckboard the road climbs and thins out to a single track between steep canyon walls. Outcrops of quartz, manganese and layers of mica shist resemble some of the material that the Buckboard shafts encountered underground and indicate the possibility of jewelry-quality rhodonite in the near vicinity.

Upon returning to the main road below the mine there is a choice of going right on a lesser-used route or continuing toward the valley on the best road. The trail to the right wanders along, in and out of small washes for a mile heading toward a mountain and turning left at a bright pink cabin of the Green Sage Mining Claims behind which is a rather large, long abandoned mine operation. Just past the cabin the route loops back toward the valley and crosses the better road in one-and-a-half miles. Straight ahead or north brings one back to the Sunshine ruins and oil surfaced road.

For more exploring take the right hand branch at this crossroad and head for the skeleton of a metal-covered mill building. This is the edge of the Atolia tungsten field which overlapped into the Stringer gold and tungsten deposit. This is a rather unique camp spot, away from traffic yet close to a road. The building stands empty and gaunt against the skyline without a hint of the sheltered places for campfires down between the mounds of tailings.

North a short distance from the building is a good road to the right that continues along a highline maintenance road through another section of the Stringer District and passes the site of the Baltic Mill, childhood home of "Desert Bonanza's" author. Side roads that can be traveled by passenger cars wind in and out of the concrete and stone foundations of mills, homes, blacksmith shops, and associated buildings that were a part of the business of claiming gold from the earth. Here are acres of treasure potential for bottle diggers and metal detector enthusiasts.

This is a popular, fairly sheltered area for winter enjoyment and camping, but is a hot, dry place with long hours of glaring heat in the summer. The main dirt road, frequented by passenger cars and campers joins the oil surfaced route to Randsburg just three tenths of a mile from the intersection of Butte and Sunshine Road. Though the car miles are surprisingly few, the Stringer area is large in its offerings for leisurely exploring.

# 10. MESQUITE CANYON ROAD

*Old mine camps, a mile-long tunnel, rock and fossil collecting, and camping spots along a good dirt road in Black Mountain country make good traveling in fall, winter, and spring.*

Some of the most picturesque desert characters of the Rand mining period traveled Mesquite Canyon enroute to their mine camps in the El Paso Range. They carved their own unique niche in history without striking a hoped-for bonanza that would have catapulted them into millionaires.

Early in the 1800's prospectors, following an old Indian foot path, worked their way up the narrow canyon searching the steep side slopes and small branching washes. Some found gold in or near the canyon while others went on to penetrate deeper into the unnamed mountains. By the 1850's the canyon was a pack route; sure-footed burros brought out gold concentrates and carried back the miner's supplies.

At the mouth of the canyon was a large cluster of mesquite trees that made it an easily identifiable spot and gave the canyon its name. A good sized stream of fresh spring water flowed toward the valley floor; grass and trees both thrived in the wet soil. It was an ideal rest area and rendezvous for miners and passing freight wagons. Gold was sent into the Los Angeles market and on the return trip the freighter would have the miner's order of food and equipment.

Every ounce of gold extracted from rock or ancient stream bed signified many hours of hard work which could be lost in a moment to ruthless outlaws. Renegades freely came and went through the canyon with no law except the miner's own ability

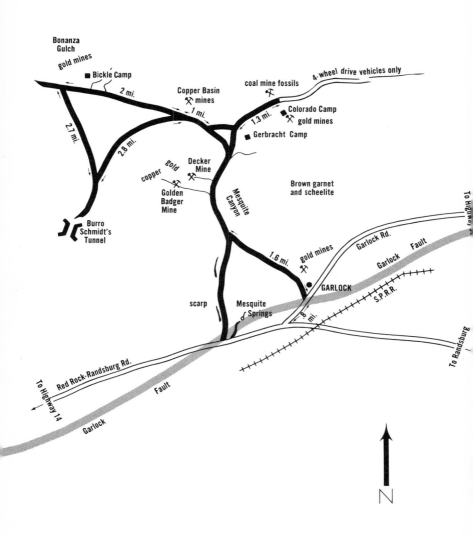

**MESQUITE CANYON ROAD**

to protect himself and his property. This state of affairs was not unique to Mesquite Canyon; it was the accepted hazard of the desert and mountains.

The outside world seldom heard of the atrocities, but occasionally, via freighters the word reached the settlements. It was in 1864 that the owner of the Yarbrough Gold and Silver Company was found murdered at Mesquite Springs while he waited with a shipment of gold concentrates. A few days later men at two mines up above Mesquite Canyon were run off and forty tons of rich gold ore, worth four hundred dollars a ton, was stolen.

Guns and highgrading were still prominent in Mesquite Canyon until a very few years ago. Many an innocent traveler looked into the yawning black depth of a gun barrel for no other reason than that he dared be in the Canyon. The Canyon that started as a pack trail and not too friendly to strangers is now quiet, residents are friendly and the road can easily be negotiated by modern passenger cars except when heavy rains or flash flooding turns the road into an escape route.

Since the canyon has become a popular access route to almost limitless mountain and valley exploration, four-wheel-drive vehicles, pickups and bikes soon recondition any areas cut by rains and all type vehicles can safely travel the entire length of the canyon. There are no sharp curves or sand traps and only a couple of short, low gear grades. It is by no means a speedway but at a leisurely pace, avoiding gravel-piled shoulders and parking on solid ground, this canyon takes the explorer into the back country for a day or as long as his schedule will permit.

There are two entrances to Mesquite Canyon within two miles of each other. For the best view of an unusual geological formation, it is advisable to go in at the south end of the historic site of Garlock and come out at the famed Mesquite Springs. The unmarked, well-used, dirt road leaves the hard surfaced Garlock road just south of the last delapidated cabin in the old town site and climbs to the north into the El Paso Mountains.

Within a little more than a mile the Mesquite Springs branch joins the Garlock road and the route gently dips to the canyon floor. Prospect holes are a frequent sight along the mountain slope and a short hike up any of the side washes will reveal others. Most are only a few feet deep where the prospector found "color" and dug a short way in hopes that it would develop into a sizeable gold deposit. He usually quit when ore indications pinched out or completely disappeared.

Two miles from the junction of the Mesquite Springs road, a foot trail goes to the left up a narrow wash. A few feet around the bend in the wash is the old Golden Badger which produced unknown amounts of gold with only a record in 1940 of $4,000 for the year. For the rock collector there are showy seams of azurite and malachite in a nearby vein of copper bearing quartz.

The next wash on the left has a narrow, eroded old wagon road, across which has been strung a cable. The road goes up a steep incline to the Decker diggings. It is a most interesting place to visit but only for those able and willing to climb the almost perpendicular half mile. Decker has long been gone, the old cabin is falling down, his dry washers, made of apple boxes and scrap lumber are deteriorating. Most of the old consumption remedy bottles are gone, that used to be in piles back of the cabin.

Decker's cabin, like many other miner's shacks, was built near the mouth of his mine on the discard dump which was the only level place in the wash. Unlike other camps, this miner gouged a zigzag open-top tunnel in the opposite direction from the mine opening. The tunnel ends abruptly in a most unique sanitary facility on the side of the mountains, with rock walls, rock floor, rock seat and blue sky for the roof.

Decker's claims like many others on the same side of the canyon have not been worked for years, even the names have been forgotten except by old timers who still recall that the Side Hill Wedge should have produced better, or that the Old Look Out probably gave up more gold than any outsider ever knew about. There was the Golden Eagle, Twin Brothers, Still Lower Half, McGowan's Gold, all silent ghosts of a long ago mining period.

A mile farther on the Mesquite road tops a ridge and the view is spectacular! Massive Black Mountain with multi-toned, eroded sides, lies straight ahead. To the left is a teasing glimpse of Last Chance Canyon and a distant panorama in blues, grays and lavenders as the Sierras stretch into the distance.

A good road to the right is only a service road to a microwave station and deadends shortly. Keep straight ahead past the sign designating Gerbracht Camp for about one hundred yards and then take the road to the right which swings around the camp. For many years the name Gerbracht struck a note of fear in those who traveled the area. To local residents she was known as Della, respected for her knowledge and collection of minerals, disliked for her habit of grabbing mine claims, and feared for the gun she carried and used. When a shot came out of nowhere, and whined too close for comfort there was usually little doubt as to who was attempting to scare one out of the canyon.

As the years went on Della became more possessive of the canyons and the El Paso range; innocent travelers were shot at and shot. The few remaining miners carried guns and told of having a feeling of being watched as they moved in and out of the canyon. Della is now gone and today's visitors can travel unmolested.

The road from the Gerbracht Camp east passes between Black Mountain on the left and rolling, vegetation covered mountains on the right. Years that there have been winter or spring rains, this area, like Mesquite Canyon, is a flower garden from March to June. Acres of white, yellow, lavender and misty pink become great waves of color as light breezes keep each flower in motion. For the student of desert flora the variety reaches from the stately Joshua to the mini-flowers at ground level with their smaller-than-pin-head size blooms.

In just over a mile the road tops a rise and the ruins of Colorado Camp lies ahead. Vandals burned the interesting old rock and wood house, knocked down the bunk houses, destroyed or carried away mine and well equipment but it is still an interesting place to explore.

Years ago copper and gold veins were developed southeast of the camp; some shafts reaching a depth of over two hundred feet. The main shafts, Copper King and the Golden Imp were rumored to be rich but how rich was never a matter of record. Here lived "Frenchie," another of the colorful individuals that traveled Mesquite Canyon. For years he carried a gun as insurance against the Gerbracht threat and carried a sizeable gold nugget to coax the unwary into investing in his gold mine.

Frenchie, in a battered pick up with his spotted dog Bowser, was a frequent and familiar sight going in and out of Mesquite Canyon. He was the El Paso Mountains con-man supreme though not unique in the mining world. When he was broke the gold nugget was sure to appear along with mining conversation. An eager investor would soon have verbal ownership, from one tenth to one half interest, in a gold mine. The extent of the investor's share depended upon his generosity. Probably no other gold mine in the Mojave Desert had as many half owners.

Though Frenchie's cabin is gone and the once neat yard now a mess of junk, brought in since the old miner departed this world, there is still one lone stand of Carizzo grass. Once abundant near desert springs it is now nearly extinct. Near the old pump house is a cluster of wild almond bushes that have survived. The scraggy, gray bush, a native of the area has small pink blooms in the spring that sends a perfume message out to every wild bee within miles. In fall the nuts furnish a tasty feast for the ground squirrels, mice and pack rats.

Across the road from Colorado Camp a bulldozed cut reveals tan slate, rich red iron stain and gray to black chunks of coal. In 1898 two hundred tons of low grade coal was mined here in three different shafts. It is reported to have been used locally to operate mining equipment and smelter operation. In the early 1900's the Southern Pacific is said to have bought a sizeable amount and hauled it out to Mojave only to find it would hardly burn much less produce enough heat needed to operate their steam locomotives.

The shafts caved in long ago and only coal that weathers out to the surface indicates where the operation existed. A search of the slate associated with the coal deposit will produce fossil casts of ancient tree limbs and leaves. Fern leaves are reputed to have been found at the one hundred and fifty foot depth during the mining operation; a search of the surface coal could be worth while for a collector.

Passenger cars should not go beyond Colorado Camp as the road develops sharp dips, high centers and ends above a deep cut in a short distance. Four wheel drive vehicles can continue on for some distance by dropping down into a wash and squeezing past overhanging cliffs and narrow cuts. The view of Black Mountain from the camp site shows a jeep trail to the foot of the mountain and a foot path winding toward the top. For the hiker there are fossil wood and agate to collect; Indian trails, house rings and arrow chips are scattered along the way.

Back track the short distance to within a few yards of the Gerbracht Camp sign, keeping to the right, head west. In about one mile a large silver-toned mine dump appears on the hill to the right across a wash. This area is known as the Copper Basin and the dump came from one of Burro Schmidt's mines. Opposite the dump and on the left side of the road is a small dug out area that once was the site of Schmidt's winter cabin. At his death the cabin was torn to shreds by friends searching for his buried gold.

Take the road to the left at the sign "Tunnel" and make the gradual climb to the top of the mountain where Schmidt had his summer cabin and dug a tunnel that placed him in Ripley's Believe It Or Not. The road is good and in less than three miles you are at the top of the mountain and being greeted by Tonie Sieger, the present owner. There is a yard full of odds and ends, Schmidt's old cabin full of artifacts from his many mining years, and his mile long tunnel to explore.

Burro Schmidt came to California, in 1894, for his health. The hot, dry desert air was the right answer. Though frail appearing he accomplished the monumental job of digging a tunnel through a mountain by hand. Sometimes he had burros or mules to pull ore cars of material to dump but most the time he not only did all the drilling, dynamiting, shoveling but at the end of the day pushed the car of rubble to the entrance of his tunnel, making the level area used for parking today. No one really knows why he spent half a life time digging a tunnel through a mountain, but there are many rumors. One rumor persists that there is a secret, sealed room off of the tunnel that is filled with gold from all his years of mining.

Coming back down the mountain side from the Burro Schmidt camp, take a left branch after leaving gateway of poles in barrels. Approximately three miles from the camp the road dead ends into Last Chance Canyon road at a sign telling about the tunnel. This dead end faces Bonanza Gulch noted for the number of rich placer claims and the place where nuggets are still found. Upper Bonanza Gulch and Last Chance Canyon are another exploratory trip, so turn right, past Bickles Camp, heading east. A canyon to the left goes to Mesa Springs, once an Indian camp site around a water source; the road is rough and for four wheel vehicles only.

A tenth-of-a-mile farther on is a passable road to the left that dead ends at a small primitive camp site. A tenth-of-a-mile farther along the main road is another trail to the left which goes into a larger camp area. This site has room for a number of campers without crowding. Unusual "mud-ball" formations add interest, old gold diggings are safe to explore and the wash offers gold panning or dry washing possibilities. It is a great place for children to run, climb and play miner in the shallow old diggings. What the early miner called these diggings has been lost through the years, but years ago we named it our Sandstone Cove, where it is pleasant even on the windiest, coldest winter day.

Go back to the main road the way you came in; the short cut to the left is sandy. Continue left or east and in less than two miles you are back at the Gerbracht Camp sign, turn right to Mesquite Canyon. In three-and-a-half miles the canyon road drops toward the valley and the right branch at the "Y" brings you out of the canyon through what geologists call "grabens." This is an ancient deposit of light colored, finely pulverized rock, now deeply eroded and topped by darker float. This is an unusual view of the result of vertical motion along the Garlock Fault. The fault itself runs about where the canyon road meets the hard surfaced Red Rock-Randsburg Road. From here Highway 395 is to the left and Highway 14 to the right.

# II. HOW TO ENJOY DESERT EXPLORING

*To enjoy your desert ghost town travels to the fullest, make sure you keep these things in mind.*

There are a few things that are insurance for a pleasant, worry-free desert experience. First of all bring your common sense along and keep it where you can put it to use at any time.

Just as one does for any trip, let the family and friends know where you plan to explore and about when to expect you home.

Stay on traveled roads unless your vehicle is built for off the road travel and in case of a breakdown stay with your vehicle. Chances are good that another explorer will be along in a short time. Cross country hikes in a strange area, desert or not, is just asking for trouble.

Dress comfortably and take along extra warm items regardless of the time of year; desert nights are cool and there can be a wide temperature variation in a short period. Walking boots have many advantages over shoes.

Carry an extra big drink of water for you and your vehicle; desert dry air increases thirst.

Take along more food than you can imagine eating, but don't be surprised if you consume it all; fresh air and exploring builds an appetite.

Keep your gas tank filled and check your spare tire for air. Service stations are not on every corner and a spare tire that has lost air through months of disuse can spoil your day.

Desert roads are not freeways, cut your speed, loaf along, see, feel and breath in the wonders of this world of many miles, varied faces and hidden values.

The desert is wonderful or dreadful, beautiful or bleak, exciting or dull —depending on you.

110

# BIBLIOGRAPHY

Bailey, Richard C. *Exploration in Kern,* Bakersfield, California: Kern County Historical Society, 1959.

Beebe, Lucius. *Mixed Train Daily,* New York: Dalton and Company, 1953.

Burmeister, Eugene. *Early Days in Kern.* Bakersfield, California: Cordon House, 1963.

Caughey, John and Laree. *California Heritage,* Los Angeles, California: The Ward Ritchie Press, 1962.

Fenton, Carrol Lane and Mildred Adams, *The Fossil Book,* New York: Doubleday and Company, 1958.

Gudde, Erwin G. *California Place Names,* Berkeley, California: University of California Press, 1965.

Jaegar, Edmund C. *The California Desert,* Stanford, California: Stanford University Press, 1965.

*Kern County Centennial Almanac,* Bakersfield, California: Kern County Centennial Observance Committee, 1966.

Leadabrand, Russ. *A Guidebook to the Mojave Desert of California,* Los Angeles, California: The Ward Ritchie Press, 1966.

Leadabrand, Russ. *Exploring California Byways, Desert Country,* Los Angeles, California: The Ward Ritchie Press, 1969.

Munz, Philip A. *California Desert Wildflowers,* Berkeley, California: University of California Press, 1962.

Nadeau, Remi. *Ghost Towns and Mining Camps of California,* Los Angeles, California: The Ward Ritchie Press, 1967.

Peirson, Emma. *Kern's Desert,* Bakersfield, California: Kern County Historical Society, 1956.

Shelton, John S. *Geology Illustrated,* San Francisco, California: W. H. Freeman Company, 1966.

Starry, Roberta M. *Golden Gamble,* China Lake, California: Maturango Museum (in publication).

Troxel, B. W. and Morton, P. K. *Mines and Mineral Resources of Kern County, California,* San Francisco, California: California Division of Mines and Geology, 1962.

Twisselmann, Earnest C. *A Flora of Kern County, California,* San Francisco, California: University of San Francisco, 1967.

Vanders, Iris and Kerr, Paul F. *Mineral Recognition,* New York: John Wiley and Sons Inc., 1967.

Wright, Laura and Troxel, B. W. *Geology of Southern California, Western Mojave Desert and Death Valley Region,* San Francisco, California: Division of Mines, 1954.

Wynn, Marcia Rittenhouse. *Desert Bonanza,* Los Angeles, California: Arthur H. Clark Company, 1963.

# INDEX

112

# $1.95 EACH—WESTERN TRAVEL & LEISURE GUIDEBOOKS FROM THE WARD RITCHIE PRESS

## Trips for the Day, Weekend or Longer

**MOST BOOKS HAVE PHOTOGRAPHS AND MAPS.**

QUANTITY | | TOTAL
---|---|---
☐ | **BACKYARD TREASURE HUNTING** | $ _____
☐ | **BAJA CALIFORNIA:** Vanished Missions, Lost Treasures, Strange Stories True and Tall | $ _____
☐ | **BICYCLE TOURING IN LOS ANGELES** | $ _____
☐ | **EAT,** A Toothsome Tour of L.A.'s Specialty Restaurants | $ _____
☐ | **EXPLORING BIG SUR, MONTEREY AND CARMEL** | $ _____
☐ | **EXPLORING CALIFORNIA BYWAYS, No. 2,** In and Around Los Angeles | $ _____
☐ | **EXPLORING CALIFORNIA BYWAYS, No. 3,** Desert Country | $ _____
☐ | **EXPLORING CALIFORNIA BYWAYS, No. 4,** Mountain Country | $ _____
☐ | **EXPLORING CALIFORNIA BYWAYS, No. 5,** Historic Sites of California | $ _____
☐ | **EXPLORING CALIFORNIA BYWAYS, No. 6,** Owens Valley | $ _____
☐ | **EXPLORING CALIFORNIA BYWAYS, No. 7,** An Historical Sketchbook | $ _____
☐ | **EXPLORING CALIFORNIA FOLKLORE** | $ _____
☐ | **EXPLORING THE GHOST TOWN DESERT** | $ _____
☐ | **EXPLORING HISTORIC CALIFORNIA** | $ _____
☐ | **EXPLORING THE MOTHER LODE COUNTRY** | $ _____
☐ | **EXPLORING SMALL TOWNS, No. 1**—Southern California | $ _____
☐ | **EXPLORING SMALL TOWNS, No. 2**—Northern California | $ _____
☐ | **EXPLORING THE UNSPOILED WEST, Vol. 1** | $ _____
☐ | **EXPLORING THE UNSPOILED WEST, Vol. 2** | $ _____
☐ | **FEET FIRST:** Walks through Ten Los Angeles Areas | $ _____
☐ | **GREAT BIKE TOURS IN NORTHERN CALIFORNIA** | $ _____
☐ | **GUIDEBOOK TO THE CANYONLANDS COUNTRY** | $ _____
☐ | **GUIDEBOOK TO THE COLORADO DESERT OF CALIFORNIA** | $ _____
☐ | **GUIDEBOOK TO THE FEATHER RIVER COUNTRY** | $ _____
☐ | **GUIDEBOOK TO THE LAKE TAHOE COUNTRY, Vol. I.** Echo Summit, Squaw Valley and the California Shore | $ _____
☐ | **GUIDEBOOK TO THE LAKE TAHOE COUNTRY, Vol. II.** Alpine County, Donner-Truckee, and the Nevada Shore | $ _____

[MORE BOOKS AND ORDER FORM ON OTHER SIDE]

| | | |
|---|---|---|
| ☐ | **GUIDEBOOK TO LAS VEGAS** | $ _____ |
| ☐ | **GUIDEBOOK TO LOST WESTERN TREASURE** | $ _____ |
| ☐ | **GUIDEBOOK TO THE MISSIONS OF CALIFORNIA** | $ _____ |
| ☐ | **GUIDEBOOK TO THE MOUNTAINS OF SAN DIEGO AND ORANGE COUNTIES** | $ _____ |
| ☐ | **GUIDEBOOK TO THE NORTHERN CALIFORNIA COAST, VOL. I.** Highway 1 | $ _____ |
| ☐ | **GUIDEBOOK TO PUGET SOUND** | $ _____ |
| ☐ | **GUIDEBOOK TO RURAL CALIFORNIA** | $ _____ |
| ☐ | **GUIDEBOOK TO THE SACRAMENTO DELTA COUNTRY** | $ _____ |
| ☐ | **GUIDEBOOK TO THE SAN BERNARDINO MOUNTAINS OF CALIFORNIA,** Including Lake Arrowhead and Big Bear | $ _____ |
| ☐ | **GUIDEBOOK TO THE SAN GABRIEL MOUNTAINS OF CALIFORNIA** $ _____ | |
| ☐ | **GUIDEBOOK TO SALTWATER FISHING IN SOUTHERN CALIFORNIA** | $ _____ |
| ☐ | **GUIDEBOOK TO THE SPAS OF NORTHERN CALIFORNIA** | $ _____ |
| ☐ | **GUIDEBOOK TO VANCOUVER ISLAND** | $ _____ |
| ☐ | **HIKING THE SANTA BARBARA BACKCOUNTRY** | $ _____ |
| ☐ | **SABRETOOTH CATS AND IMPERIAL MAMMOTHS** | $ _____ |
| ☐ | **SKI LOS ANGELES** | $ _____ |
| ☐ | **WHERE TO TAKE YOUR CHILDREN IN NEVADA** | $ _____ |
| ☐ | **WHERE TO TAKE YOUR CHILDREN IN NORTHERN CALIFORNIA** | $ _____ |
| ☐ | **WHERE TO TAKE YOUR CHILDREN IN SOUTHERN CALIFORNIA** | $ _____ |
| ☐ | **WHERE TO TAKE YOUR GUESTS IN SOUTHERN CALIFORNIA** | $ _____ |
| ☐ | **YOUR LEISURE TIME . . . HOW TO ENJOY IT** | $ _____ |

**THE WARD RITCHIE PRESS**
474 S. Arroyo Parkway, Pasadena, Calif. 91105

Please send me the Western Travel and Leisure Guidebooks I have checked. I am enclosing $_____ (check or money order). Please include 25¢ per copy to cover mailing costs. California residents add state sales tax.

Name _____

Address _____

City _____ State _____ Zip Code _____